A simple guide to

searching the Internet

Gilles Fouchard &
Rob Young

An imprint of PEARSON EDUCATION

Pearson Education Limited

Head Office:
Edinburgh Gate
Harlow
Essex CM20 2JE
Tel: +44 (0)1279 623623
Fax: +44 (0)1279 431059

London Office:
128 Long Acre
London WC2E 9AN
Tel: +44 (0)20 7447 2000
Fax: +44 (0)20 7240 5771
Website: www.informit.uk.com

This edition published in Great Britain in 2001. © Pearson Education Limited 2001

First published in 1999 as
Recherche sur Internet –
se former un Jour
by CampusPress France,
19, rue Michel Le Comte, 75003
Paris, France.

ISBN 0-130-60280-9

British Library Cataloguing-in-Publication Data
A catalogue record for this book can be obtained from the British Library.

10 9 8 7 6 5 4 3 2 1

Typeset by Pantek Arts Ltd, Maidstone, Kent.
Printed and bound in Italy.

The Publisher's policy is to use paper manufactured from sustainable forests.

Contents

5 Directories of people and companies

10 Searching the media

11 'Push' technologies

Introduction

Imagine you're looking for someone's phone number. You pick up your local phone directory, flick through it, and... it's not in alphabetical order! Still, no problem. You know the number's in there somewhere, so you can just keep looking until you find it.

It probably doesn't sound like much fun. Searching through a few pages isn't too bad, but the entire directory? Fortunately that's not how the phone book works. Unfortunately, though, it is how the Internet works.

The whole of human knowledge and experience is out there somewhere, but where do you find the tiny bit of it you're looking for? It isn't organised into any kind of structure; new pages and Web sites aren't automatically listed in some central directory, and there's no system for cataloguing what particular pages are about or what words they contain. What the Internet does have is hundreds of search tools to help you sort through this jumble of information. Just pick the right tool, ask it the right question, and you'll find what you were looking for quickly and painlessly.

Of course, now you need to know *which* of those hundreds of tools is the best one to use for a particular type of information, and how to phrase the question to be sure of finding the answer. That's the point of this book. Knowing how to search the Internet effectively can save you minutes or even hours. With the

Internet continuing to grow at an amazing rate, it could soon mean the difference between finding what you need and *not* finding it!

How to use this book

Like most things in life, searching the Internet is simple *when you know how to do it*. By starting from Chapter 1 and following each chapter you'll progress from the basics to advanced search skills in a structured way. But you don't have to know everything about searching to start improving the results you get: each chapter contains self-contained information, so you can skip about the book all you like.

Throughout the book you'll see icons in the margins. These indicate notes that provide extra detail, introduce a new idea, or explain a technical term that we couldn't avoid using. The icon used tells you what sort of information the note contains:

This icon introduces handy shortcuts and tips such as keyboard hotkeys, expert options, and quicker ways of getting to the same place.

This icon warns you of any risks associated with a particular action, or any problems you might encounter along the way, and (where possible) shows you how to avoid them.

This icon is used to provide additional information about the topic being covered.

Basic skills

1

People usually measure the Internet and its growth in terms of the number of users. With over 300 million surfers throughout the world, and around 1 million new users every month, the Internet is a phenomenon which cannot be ignored. Its content (number of sites, number of Web pages) is also growing at a phenomenal rate. In June 2000 there were 18 million registered Web addresses, compared with 6 million just one year earlier. And the number of domain names is an indication of the number of sites set up on the Web: 13 million in June 2000 compared with 4 million a year earlier. You can imagine the effect of this on the number of Web pages! With such exponential growth, the Web is becoming a veritable labyrinth through which it is difficult to find one's way. Whether a novice or an experienced surfer, you need to use search tools in order to make effective use of the Internet.

In order to achieve what you set out to do, avoiding time wasted surfing aimlessly, it is necessary to use the best tools offered on the Internet in general and the Web in particular. At your service you have search engines, directories, help features, selections, metasearch engines and 'searchbots'. As you will see in this book, there are plenty of good tools. So you will need to make the right choice and then you will need to learn how to use these tools. Among this plethora of tools, the search engine is of unimagined power for the beginner. Experienced surfers will also be able to refine their technique and learn how to select the right tools, optimise searches and interpret results.

Searching the Internet is empirical in nature. You can either work strictly in order to achieve your goal without any detours, or you can proceed by means of trial and error in order to uncover the odd pearl. It is by searching that you learn to search, so don't hesitate to try things out, to overlap requests and to refine your methods and how you express yourself as you progress.

What is a search engine?

For anybody who has already ventured onto the Web, this question does not arise. The search tool on the Internet is as indispensable as a library's catalogue, or the index of an encyclopaedia.

On the Web there are millions of pages and billions of words to be indexed. Like any document, a Web page may be indexed in two different ways:

- using keywords defining the page or document;
- using full text mode indexing.

In the first case, you can, for example, find all the pages relating to 'Tourism' (it is the page author who has indicated the keyword, or a professional surfer who has placed this page in this category). In the second case, you will have access to all pages containing the word 'tourism'.

A search engine therefore indexes Internet objects (sites, Web pages, images, etc.). This strength is doubled by the updating of these indexes. Hundreds of sites are being created around the world every day and in line with this the content of indexes needs to be updated regularly.

To do this, the larger search engines work automatically and analyse the Internet in order to discover new sites and update their pages.

Here again, several methods of updating are used:

- automatic updating using a Web-trawling program called a 'spider';
- updating of a site by the author who simultaneously registers his pages in a given engine;

Are search engines infallible?

The answer is obviously 'no'. Most engines do not interpret articles such as 'a', 'an' or 'the'. Thus a search relating to the rock group 'The Who' may give surprising results!

It is therefore necessary to make the right choice, supplement your request using Boolean operators (more on these later) or search by category in order to achieve your aims.

■ manual updating by professional surfers and cyber-journalists, whose job it is to hunt down new sites and update databases.

Each method has its advantages. Of course, the spider application can do a lot of work. Engines such as Infoseek, Excite or HotBot boast of having indexed millions of pages! But power does not always mean quality, as the more pages the engine has labelled, the more specific your request must be, otherwise you will be overwhelmed by an overabundance of lists of results. Fortunately, engines can also evaluate the results provided and, in this case, can retrieve lists in order of relevance. But how do you evaluate the relevance of each search engine?

Sometimes you may prefer manual selection by professionals. In addition, you may attribute great value to guides provided by cyber-journalists who give their opinion of sites visited and prepare classifications. In this way automated and human methods complement one another.

What does a search engine consist of?

Whether you are a novice on the Web or a pro, search engines constitute your privileged point of entry to the Web. And there is no better way to understand how they work and to demystify the subject than to examine closely how they operate.

Apart from the distinction between UK-specific search engines and the more general search engines that can lead you to Web sites throughout the world, we can loosely group search engines into the following categories:

■ those which spend their time indexing Web pages, such as Excite, AltaVista or HotBot;

- those which organise and grade information under headings and subheadings and constitute huge directories (such as Yahoo!, which has both worldwide and UK-specific versions);
- those which also evaluate and comment on the sites visited, such as Magellan, provided by the McKinley company.

As we have stated already, there are many techniques used to build search engines and directories:

- automated location and indexing;
- use of manual recording by Web site designers and editors;
- recording and possibly evaluation of sites by teams of independent surfers.

Indexing Web pages and sites

There are a number of search tools which combine these various possibilities. Search engines that use automatic 'spider' applications can create indexes of millions of pages, e.g. more than 250 million in the case of engines like AltaVista. In fact, current techniques allow around 9 million pages to be indexed each day, allowing the entire index to be refreshed once a month. However, the number of pages indexed is not the essential indicator of an engine's quality.

Furthermore, indexing methods vary greatly from one engine to another. The criteria making it possible to differentiate the techniques used are as follows:

- regularity of updating;
- processing time of pages retrieved for indexing;
- nature of data indexed: text, images, etc.

The components of a search engine
A search engine consists of several components:

The 'spider' or 'crawler' is in charge of connecting with Web servers, visiting sites, reading pages and following the links on these pages within the same site. The 'spider' must go to the site regularly in order to note any changes. A gigantic task!

Everything that the 'spider' finds will be used to compile the index, the second component. Look at the index of this book in order to see the benefits of an index. The most advanced techniques are used to design the indexes of Web sites and pages. The index is regularly updated by adding, deleting or amending entries. But there is still a time lapse between reality, what the spider has been able to detect and this actually being recorded in the index.

The search engine itself is the third component. It is this which analyses the request you enter when you visit the search site, refers to the index to find matching pages and prepares the results. It is also this which has the task of sorting the results in order of relevance before presenting them to you.

Browsing and searching
Bearing in mind the difficult nature of the task (i.e. indexing sites and providing quality results to millions of surfers), no engine can claim to be exhaustive, or to perform the best, or to be infallible in the results transmitted. What is required is speed and reliability. It is easy to see that the operation of a search engine and the techniques used are a matter of compromise.

Performance varies from one system to another and depends on the nature of the search carried out. Each system has its strengths and weaknesses, and at times several engines need to be used in order to overlap and refine searches.

In general, each search engine offers:

- simple searches by keywords;
- complex searches using Boolean operators (AND/OR/NOT) and specific commands;
- searches by subject or site category.

Depending on the performance of the helper application used, the search may be easy or difficult. You must get to know the strengths and weaknesses of each search engine, which sometimes depend on the nature of the search undertaken.

Evaluating results

A search engine's performance lies in its capacity to interpret the request, evaluate the documents found and classify search results (hits). This usually involves allocating a percentage indicating how closely the hit matches your search term, and avoids the lengthy consultation of huge lists of results. The first sites proposed are deemed to best answer the enquiry. Again, this depends on the engine correctly interpreting the request made (the search term used).

You will be able to see that search engines work very fast most of the time, but their results often include sites or pages which are not of interest. It is up to you to sort the good from the bad!

In their defence, it must be acknowledged that search engines are not able to ask you additional questions in order to make their search more specific. It is up to you to take the initiative and if necessary word the request differently. Nor can they become enriched by your questions, although these are experiences which they could record in order to improve with time. We only know that search engines keep track of requests made in order to provide statistics which are of interest to surfers. We also know that search engines interpret the nature of requests in order to return advertising banners relating to them. In short, they are not as stupid as you might think. You can count on the creativity of programmers to constantly include more intelligence in these helper applications.

Again in their defence, search engines are tireless workers and do not draw back from anything. You can tell them 'Tourism' and they will send you thousands of pages of results. Try to ask a librarian the same thing and there is a good chance that you will be asked to be more specific, if not sent packing!

So what do search engines do to establish degrees of relevance in the results sent back to you?

First of all they use the **location/frequency method**. In plain English, they use rules which interpret the position of the words found and their frequency. The word 'Tourism' will have more weight in the title of a page than in the Web page itself. It is the number of times the word appears in the page itself which will eventually decide between two pages where the keyword appears in the title.

The position of a word in the page is also relevant. Thus, the engine can determine whether the word in question appears at the top of the page, in a title or in the first paragraph, all of which will have more weight than its appearance at the bottom of the page.

Most engines use this basic method with their own variations. That is why, among other things, different engines will produce different results for the same request.

As we have said, Internet search engines are far from equal:

- some record more pages than others;
- some update their index faster;
- some are more efficient than others.

Other methods of differentiation are used by search engines. For example, WebCrawler tests the **popularity of links**. It will give preference to a page to which lots of links point rather than to a page which fewer sites have linked to.

We can also assume that directory-based search engines will give better scores to sites that have been reviewed by the search site's own reviewer. A site visited by a professional team will be preferred to sites that are unknown.

Indexing from meta tags

So far we have made no mention of an important ingredient in Web page indexing: **meta tags**. What are these? Meta tags are hidden programming codes which are used by programmers to describe a Web site or page and record the associated keywords. These commands are used because engines interpret them. So far so good, since meta tags were dreamed up precisely to facilitate indexing and further searches. It is by using these commands skillfully that the programmer will be able to ensure that his page is 'retrieved' by search engines.

While some search engines, such as Excite, ignore the keywords recorded in meta tags, others, such as HotBot, make great use of them. Nowadays, though, few search engines rely on meta tags entirely because they are so open to misuse. A Web author keen to see his site ranked highly may try to 'fool' the engine. Starting from the assumption that there is a great demand for erotic sites, an author might include words like 'nudity' in his meta tags to ensure that his page appears in the results for that type of search — even if the site contains nothing more than pictures of classical Greek statues!

The designers of Web pages and sites have several ways of getting themselves known by indexing applications:

- *site title;*
- *site description: this is a hidden programming code (a tag in HTML) containing the site description given by the editor or author; or*
- *keywords: this is another hidden code which contains a list of keywords attributed to sites.*

Today, everyone is free to describe a site as he chooses, and in the long run this is what can create anomalies in 'hits' (search results).

Search engines are wise to this, of course, and they try to filter out this type of abuse. If a word is repeated a hundred or so times one after the other to try to win the 'frequency' competition, the engine may decide to ignore the site completely. Another popular trick, to win points for 'location', is to include lists of keywords in the first paragraph of a page, but to make that paragraph invisible to the reader by making its text colour match the background so that only the search engine will see them.

Since meta tags are absolutely freely defined, it is inevitable that engines will make mistakes in their interpretation. While the Excite solution of ignoring meta tags altogether is protective, it may penalise strict authors. The ideal solution would be to create a description standard accepted at the highest level, a standard on which engines could depend. Doubtless this will come. In the meantime, cyberspace, like the real world, is an imperfect world.

Presenting results

Indexing pages and analysing requests are the basic tasks of the search engine but it still has to display the results as comprehensively as possible for the surfer. Here, too, methods vary from one engine to another. Every kind of site description corresponding to a request may be displayed:

- the descriptions incorporated in meta tags;
- Web page titles;
- the first lines of a Web page;
- the review of the site by the search engine's own team;
- the page address (URL);
- the page size;

- the date of the last update;
- the degree of relevance.

Searching the Internet: principles

While some search sites offer you a range of options (drop-down lists, check-boxes, and so on), others leave you to construct your search query yourself and type it into a text-field. Before we look at the different options available, remember that all search engines have Help pages explaining how they work. Although there's no standardised syntax for search queries, many engines offer similar options and follow similar rules: these Help pages will help you find the differences and point out any extra features you can use that may be useful in a particular type of search.

The AltaVista search engine, for example, uniquely allows you to search for images or Java applets on a page, or search in site URLs, amongst other things. Other engines may have (or may add in the future) other options which may not be obvious until you look at their Help pages.

Match any or Match all?
When you type several keywords in the search box, two things may occur:

- The engine searches for pages containing *all* the keywords (the 'Match All' option, used by HotBot, Lycos and Go.com)
- The engine searches for pages containing *at least* one of the words (the 'Match Any' option, used by AltaVista, Excite and WebCrawler)

continued

For the curious, this is how meta tags are coded in HTML language:

```
<META     NAME="key-
words"    CONTENT="
cuisine, gastronomy,
soil, wine">
```

```
<META NAME="descrip-
tion"     CONTENT="A
magazine on tradi-
tional cooking, good
wine and the fruit
of the soil.'>
```

And for engines that ignore meta tags there are still comments:

```
<!--A magazine  on
traditional   cook-
ing, good wines and
the  fruit  of  the
soil.-->
```

The site address, or URL (Uniform Resource Locator), is also used in searches. Although it's not the most usual starting point for a search, some engines do offer it as an option. Thus addresses including keywords may be searched for or a search may be restricted to a specific domain.

In the latter case, the number of words found may be one of the relevant criteria. The engine will display at the top the pages where it has found all the words. For the others it will indicate the number of words found, e.g. 2/4.

Bearing in mind these differences in behaviour, this is how each of the families of engine manages to respond to requests:

- to obtain 'Match any' with HotBot, for example, you must use the menu command options or code the request using the OR operator: 'Tourism OR England';
- to obtain 'Match all' with AltaVista, for example, you must use the operators + or AND: 'Tourism + England' or 'Tourism AND England'.

Boolean operators

Boolean operators are used to express logical search conditions. The two basic operators are AND and OR. While the AND operator is unambiguous, OR can take two forms:

The normal OR: in a search for 'A OR B' the page can contain A only, B only, or both A and B to be regarded as a match.

The exclusive OR: in a search for 'A OR B' the page can contain either A or B, but not both, to be regarded as a match.

Only the normal OR is used by default in search engines.

Exclusion

All engines allow you to exclude a word from results. If you are interested in tourism outside the UK, you can exclude the word 'UK'. Nothing complicated, except that the syntax varies from one engine to another.

- the – sign is used with AltaVista or Lycos;
- AND NOT is used with Infoseek, HotBot or AltaVista;
- NOT is used with WebCrawler or Lycos.

You can see from the three subtly different options above that it helps to get to know how your favourite search engines work!

Searching for sentences

The search query **Tourism and UK** does not mean the same as the query '**Tourism in UK**'. In the first case, a search is carried out relating to 3 keywords, probably with non-interpretation of the word 'and' by the search engine. In the second case, pages including the precise sentence 'Tourism in UK' are searched for.

Most engines use double quotes for this, or offer a choice via a menu (Excite or HotBot).

Upper and lower case

Only use capital letters in a search if you expect to *find* capital letters. If you're not concerned whether the word you're searching for is found capitalised or not, use lower case. A search for **egypt** would find instances in a page of **Egypt**, **egypt** or (in a rather unusual page!) **eGyPt**, but if you search for **Egypt** the engine will ignore any other case combinations it finds.

It follows, then, that you may be able to narrow down your search a lot if a word is frequently used in lower case but you expect to find a capital letter in the particular context you're interested in. If, for example, you wanted infor-

Remember that a Web site address is structured as follows:
http://www.server_name. domain/directory_ name/ page_name

- **http.** This is the communication protocol used, in this case HyperText Transfer Protocol; this protocol was designed for transferring Web pages (which are based on 'hypertext') around the Internet.

- **www.** Short for World Wide Web, the most popular area of the Internet. Developed in 1990, the Web makes *continued*

use of hypertext technology, i.e. the connection of pages and documents using links. On the Web, one page contains all kinds of links:

■ **Links in the same page**. *These are also called anchors. They make it possible to move quickly around a large text document (one page).*

■ **Links with another page of the same site.** *These links are used to move from one page to another within the same site. They allow the user to navigate the site.*

■ **Links with a page of another site.** *These links are offered*

mation about a town called Bucket, you could search for it with a capital 'B' and your search results should contain few links to pages containing general 'bucket information'.

Search engines such as Go.com treat sequences of capitalised words as a phrase so that double quotes are not needed: a search for **Buckingham Palace** would automatically be regarded as a phrase, for instance, and you can search for multiple phrases like this at once by separating each phrase with a comma (such as **Prince Charles**, **Buckingham Palace**).

Proximity

Some engines allow you to indicate parameters relating to proximity between the keywords designated. For example, **A NEAR B** indicates that word A must be close to word B (used by AltaVista, Lycos, or WebCrawler).

Note that Go.com offers the command [**A B**]: words between square brackets.

You can even specify the level of proximity: **A NEAR/10 B** indicates that A and B are within 10 words of each other (used by Lycos and WebCrawler).

Wildcards

Wildcards, familiar to DOS users, are probably new to others.

This is how they work in general:

■ the * character indicates a string of characters of any length. 'Art*' thus makes it possible to search for art, artist or artisan.

■ The $ character indicates a character in a specific position.
'Artist$' carries out a search for artists (in the plural) or artiste.

Searching by field

Some engines offer particular searches by type of field:

■ the title of Web pages;
■ addresses or URL;
■ domain names;
■ links.

This is the case with AltaVista, HotBot and Infoseek in particular.

Getting started with your browser

Setting a search engine as your home page

Your Internet browser (Microsoft Internet Explorer or Netscape Communicator, the two most frequently used tools) makes it possible to set a particular Web site to be shown every time you start surfing. As most of your Web sessions could well start with searches for information or sites, you might choose to set your favourite search engine as your browser's starting page.

This is how to proceed with Internet Explorer 5.0:

1. Click on **Tools**.
2. Click on **Internet Options**.
3. Select the General tab, if necessary.

continued

by the developers of Web sites to reference other useful sites which may, of course, be on other servers (computers storing Web pages). It is possible in this way to move from one site to another, from one Web server to another and often from one country to another by just a few clicks of the mouse. The user navigates without worrying about where data is located, all that matters to him is what he is looking for.

This natural method of navigating using hyperlinks is commonly known as 'surfing the Internet'.

It is very easy to put together a query using a search engine, and the reply arrives quickly. But remember that the engine doesn't know what you're really looking for, it only knows what you've asked for! Make sure you re-read your request before submitting it, and check how the engine works, so that you can be sure that the results really will be relevant.

4. In the Home page box, enter the Internet address of the selected engine.

5. Confirm by clicking on the **Apply** button, then on **OK**.

Search tools integrated in browsers

Netscape (Communicator) and Internet Explorer have a Search button which gives access to specific search resources on the Internet.

This button in fact gives each of them access to a specific Web page which offers links with pre-selected engines.

Searching with Netscape

The Netscape Netcenter page (**http://home.netscape.com**) allows you to choose between a range of popular tools, with the Lycos search engine pushed to the fore.

Four other categories of search tool are also offered:

- search engines in the strict sense, like AltaVista, Excite, HotBot or Google (see Chapter 3);
- Web guides (searching by category): Lycos, Yahoo! (see also Chapter 3);
- yellow or white pages in order to search for companies or people (address, telephone and e-mail): Bigfoot, Infospace (see Chapter 5);
- specialist services: sale by auction, purchase and sale of vehicles.

You will also find access to a subject guide on the home page: Netscape Search at **http://search.netscape.com/**.

Be careful regarding:
- capitals;

- the use of Boolean operators and commands specific to each engine;

- the position of brackets in writing complex logical operations;

- typing errors!

Figure 1.1 Setting the popular UK Plus search engine as start page in Internet Explorer 5.0.

Searching with Internet Explorer 5.0

By clicking on the **Search** button on the toolbar of Internet Explorer 5.0, you open a search pane on the left-hand side of the screen. Just choose where you want to search, type your keywords and press Enter (or click the Search button). The available choices are:

Find a Web page: this option is selected by default, and this Web search via UK Plus is probably the one you will use the most

When you have found a search engine which suits you, display the Internet options window as above. Then click on the Use Current button to reference the page of the engine being used.

Figure 1.2 The Netscape Netcenter home page.

Previous searches: Internet Explorer tracks previous search queries you have used so that you can simply click one to search for it again

Find a map: search Microsoft's own Expedia.com site for maps

Find UK entertainment: a search of Virgin Net's guide to find films, gigs and days out

Figure 1.3 The online Netscape Search directory.

Find in newsgroups: searches for articles posted to newsgroups (covered in Chapter 6).

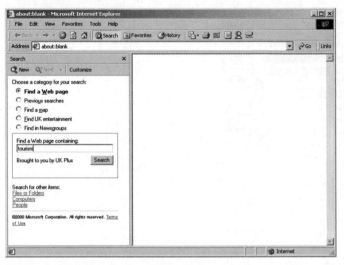

Figure 1.4 Internet Explorer's search pane.

The search results open in the same small pane, with the benefit that you can click a link to view the site it refers to in the main part of the window without losing track of the remaining results.

As with any search, you can click the **Next 10** link below the search results to view the next set of results, or click the **Next** button at the top of the search pane to run the same search with a different search engine (for UK users, there is a choice of UK Plus, Voila, Excite and MSN). To start a new search, click the **New** button at the top of the search pane.

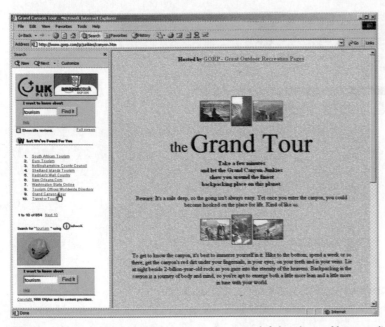

Figure 1.5 Results of a search open in the same left-hand pane. You can click a link to open it in the main window.

You can customise the options presented in the search pane by clicking the **Customize** button, although the options are limited. Essentially, you can switch off options by removing checkmarks from boxes beside them (for instance, you can prevent the **Find a map** option from being offered), or you

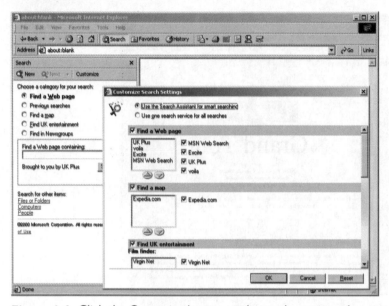

Figure 1.6 Click the Customize button to change the options shown in Internet Explorer's search pane.

can change the order in which options are presented so that your favourite search engine or option appears first in the list.

At any time, you can close the search pane by clicking the **Search** button on Internet Explorer's toolbar a second time, or by clicking the **Close** button marked with an 'X' at the top of the search pane.

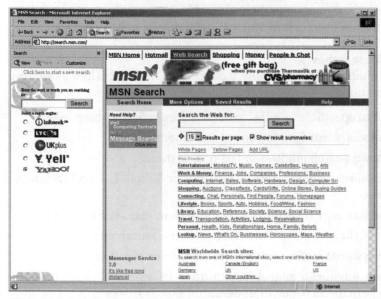

Figure 1.7 Microsoft's MSN Search page, which also makes use of the search pane.

Microsoft also offers its own search page as part of its Microsoft Network (MSN) site: go to **http://search.msn.com** for this site. If you have Internet Explorer's search pane open, you'll see it change dramatically to offer a choice between five very popular search engines: InfoSeek, Lycos, UK Plus, Yell.com and Yahoo!.

By clicking the More Options link at the top of the page you can switch to a page offering advanced search options of the type we discussed earlier in the chapter.

By selecting options from menus and checking boxes you can construct a very precise query and choose exactly how you want the results to be displayed.

9 tips for successful searches

To round off this chapter, here are nine tips to keep in mind when searching the Web for information:

1. Go from general to specific: use a fast search before refining the request.
2. Select the right tools, according to your requirements.
3. Use the well-known search engines in the first instance.
4. Use UK-specific search engines such as UK plus or Yahoo! UK and Ireland to find UK Web sites.
5. Overlap and possibly enrich results using more than one search engine.
6. Examine carefully the search options offered by the search engine.
7. Use search-by-keywords and search-by-site categories together.
8. If necessary, use advanced search techniques (power searches) and the search engine's help file in order to understand how it works.
9. Use metasearch engines for specific searches, reducing your work time.

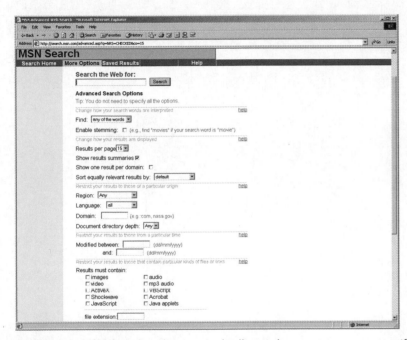

Figure 1.8 MSN Search makes it easy (well, *easier*) to construct very specific searches if you choose to.

UK search engines

2

UK versions of international search engines

UK-specific search engines

For everyday Web surfing and general research, there are large numbers of search engines available that can help you find what you're looking for. But there are times when only a UK site will do. For example, if you need legal or financial advice, want to book theatre or rail tickets, or want to check tonight's TV schedules, international search engines may not be much help. Instead, you want a search engine that's guaranteed to answer your query by providing links to UK web sites.

There is a good choice of UK search engines, falling into two categories:

- UK versions of international search engines (Yahoo! UK and Ireland, for example);
- UK-specific search engines, listing only UK sites and ignoring the rest of the Web.

UK versions of international search engines

'UK version' here means the adaptation of an international search engine (see Chapter 3) to favour UK sites. Popular search engines and directories such as Yahoo!, Lycos, InfoSeek and Excite each offer a UK version. In most cases you can choose whether to search the entire Web or just the UK portion of it, so you may choose to use the UK-specific version in preference to the international version, whatever type of information you want to find.

Yahoo! UK and Ireland
http://www.yahoo.co.uk
More than a search engine, Yahoo! UK and Ireland is a subject directory which offers searching by keywords. It does not provide its own summaries of the

sites found, but instead uses (usually very brief) site descriptions submitted by the author of a site.

On the main Yahoo! UK and Ireland page, the search choices are simple:

- **All sites:** searches the entire Yahoo! directory. UK site matches will appear at the top of the list of search results with international sites below;
- **UK & Ireland sites only:** limits the search to sites in the UK and Ireland.

Along with the keywords you want to search for, you can use inverted commas to indicate a sentence or expression, and + or – signs to include or exclude a word.

To gain a little more control over the way the search is conducted, click the **Options** link beside the Search button. From the Options page you can make more detailed selections:

- search Yahoo! (for Web sites), Usenet newsgroups or e-mail addresses;
- search for direct links to Web sites that match your keywords or for matching Yahoo! categories;
- choose to search for the exact phrase you entered, matches on all words, matches on any word, or a person's name.

On this page, you can also choose the number of hits displayed on each page of the search results, and limit the search to include only recently added sites.

Yahoo!'s search results are presented in two sections:

- **Site categories:** this is the subject hierarchy used by Yahoo!. Each category contains a number of Web sites, plus further categories that form a subset of that category (for example, Society & Culture contains a Relationships category, which itself contains a PenPals category).

■ **Web sites:** these are direct links to Web sites that match the keywords you entered. UK and Ireland sites are marked with flags to distinguish them from international sites.

Figure 2.1 The Yahoo! UK & Ireland logo.

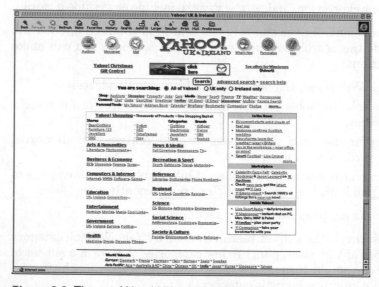

Figure 2.2 The main Yahoo! UK & Ireland search page.

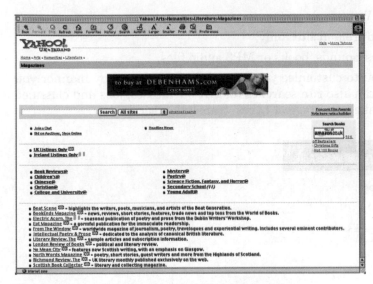

Figure 2.3 Search results from Yahoo! UK & Ireland.

Lycos UK
http://www.lycos.co.uk
Like Yahoo! UK and Ireland, the front page of Lycos UK offers a straightforward choice between searching the entire Web or limiting the search to UK and Ireland sites. The search engine returns a list of hits with a degree of relevance expressed as a percentage.

Lycos offers a range of search services on its Search Options page:

- search the entire Web;
- search for UK and Ireland sites only;
- search for pictures, sounds, books or MP3 audio files.

This page allows you to customise your search in just about any manner you could think of. You can also run searches for UK businesses, jobs and classified advertisements or take advantage of Lycos' translation service.

Figure 2.4 The Lycos logo.

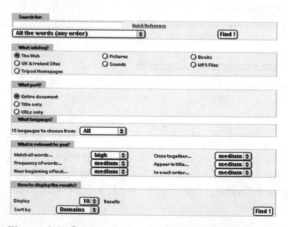

Figure 2.5 Customising your search at Lycos UK.

For each search made, Lycos keeps track of each word on each Web page listed. Common words such as 'the', 'a' and 'and' have been deleted, allowing the search to be optimised by eliminating words which are not significant. All search engines work in a similar way. However, searching for an expression such as 'To the one' may cause problems.

AltaVista United Kingdom
http://www.altavista.co.uk
AltaVista is another large international search engine with country-specific sites for a number of other countries (Germany, Sweden and India, to name but a few). Along with the usual options to search the entire Web or just the UK portion of it, a drop-down list allows searching in more than a dozen other languages.

Above the search field you'll find a row of three 'tabs'. When you first arrive at AltaVista you're on the **Search** page. By clicking the **Images**, **Audio & Video** tab, you can switch to a similar-looking page to search for multimedia files, and three option-buttons below the search field let you choose which type of multimedia files you want: images, audio or video.

Figure 2.6 The AltaVista UK logo.

The middle tab is labelled **Advanced Search**, and as you might expect, clicking this tab gives you an opportunity to use some of the Boolean search options we covered in Chapter 1. AltaVista supports the terms AND, AND NOT, OR, and NEAR, which must be entered in upper case with spaces before and after them.

Part of the power of all the AltaVista search engines (not only the UK-specific one) is their ability to search more than just the text of pages: AltaVista can search the domain name, the URL, or even the HTML code used to construct the page. These powerful options involve using a single keyword followed by a colon and the text to search for. The following 10 keywords can be used:

anchor:*search text*

Search for pages in which the *search text* appears in a clickable link to another page or site.

applet:*class name*

Search for pages that contain a Java applet named *class name*.

domain:*domain name*

Search for pages within a particular domain (such as **domain:uk** or **domain:com**).

host:*host name*

Search only on a particular server for pages (for example, **host:www.geocities.com** would find pages at www.geocities.com).

image:*file name*

Search for images named *file name* (for example, **image:apple** would find pictures named apple.gif and apple.jpg).

like:*site URL*

Search for more sites that cover similar topics to *site URL*.

link:*site URL*

Search for pages that contain links to *site URL* (you might use this to find out whether anyone is linking to your own site, for example).

text:*search text*

Search for pages that contain *search text* in a readable part of the page (not in its HTML code).

title:_search text_   Search for pages in which the title of the page contains _search text_.

url:_search text_   Search for pages in which _search text_ appears somewhere in the URL of the page (which may be the server name, one of the directories in the path, or the page's file name).

To find out more about the AltaVista keywords and their uses, click the **Help** link on the front page of any AltaVista site.

Figure 2.7 A standard search at AltaVista UK.

Excite UK
http://www.excite.co.uk

Excite is an original, powerful search engine which encourages searching by ideas and concepts rather than keywords. It uses the ICE technique (Intelligent Concept Extraction) to determine the correspondence between words and ideas. Hits are sorted according to their relevance, with the pages that best match the search criteria placed at the top of the list.

When the search results appear, a site that corresponds exactly to what you were hoping to find can be used as the basis for a more specific search. To do

Using Boolean functions with Excite

Boolean functions override Excite's concept-based searching and allow you to run searches for the exact keywords you specify. The Boolean operators available are AND, AND NOT, OR and brackets. These operators must be entered in upper case, with a space before and after them.

AND: The documents found must contain all the words linked by the AND operator. OR: The documents found must contain one of the words linked by OR.

this, just click the 'More Like This' link beside the URL. The search engine will then use this document as a reference for another search on similar sites.

Excite UK lets you search the entire Web, UK sites only, European sites or Usenet newsgroups. Check the appropriate radio button below the search field. For more precise searching, you can use the + sign to indicate words that must be included in hits and the – sign to exclude a word from the search. You can also use inverted commas to indicate phrases or sentences.

The hits produced by the Excite search engine include the percentage of relevance, the site or page title, the URL and a summary.

Along with its UK version and the international site at **www.excite.com**, Excite offers versions adapted to other languages and countries including Australia, China, Germany, Japan, Italy, France, Sweden and the Netherlands.

Figure 2.8 The Excite UK logo.

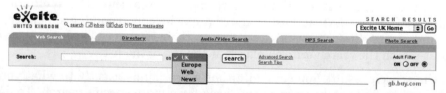

Figure 2.9 Choose whether to search the entire Web, UK sites, European sites or newsgroups.

Describe what you want to find...

I want to search	English ⬦
In the following domains	UK Sites ⬦
My search results MUST contain	the word(s) ⬦
My search results MUST NOT contain	the word(s) ⬦
My search results CAN contain	the word(s) ⬦
⦿ Display my results by document with	titles & summaries ⬦ and 10 ⬦ results per page.
○ Display the top 40 results grouped by web site.	

TIP: Do NOT use quotation marks, modifiers like '+' and '–' or operators like 'AND' in this form.
A phrase is a group of two or more words that form a unit based on the exact order in which they appear, e.g. seven wonders of the world

[Search]

Figure 2.10 Selecting words to add to an Excite search.

LookSmart United Kingdom
http://www.looksmart.co.uk

LookSmart is a directory-based search engine that uses 'categories' in much the same way as Yahoo!. LookSmart comes from the same stable as the popular and powerful international search engine AltaVista, and it's actually this engine which carries out your searches.

The LookSmart search interface is fast and simple: just type in your keywords and click the **Go!** button. Like Yahoo!, LookSmart presents links to matching categories first, followed by links to Web pages that match your search terms. The Web page results give the title of the page or site, a brief description and a link to the LookSmart category in which that site was found, allowing you to browse the category for links to similar sites.

Figure 2.11 The LookSmart logo.

continued

AND NOT: The documents found must not contain the word which follows the term AND NOT.

( ): Brackets are used to join together segments of Boolean enquiries to allow even more specific searches. For example, to find documents containing the word 'fruit' and either the word 'banana' or the word 'apple', you would type 'fruit AND (banana OR apple)'.

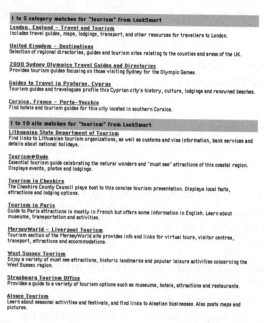

1 to 5 category matches for "tourism" from LookSmart

London, England – Travel and Tourism
Includes travel guides, maps, lodgings, transport, and other resources for travellers to London.

United Kingdom – Destinations
Selection of regional directories, guides and tourism sites relating to the counties and areas of the UK.

2000 Sydney Olympics Travel Guides and Directories
Provides tourism guides focusing on those visiting Sydney for the Olympic Games.

Guides to Travel in Protaras, Cyprus
Tourism guides and travelogues profile this Cyprian city's history, culture, lodgings and renowned beaches.

Corsica, France – Porto-Vecchio
Find hotels and tourism guides for this city located in southern Corsica.

1 to 10 site matches for "tourism" from LookSmart

Lithuanian State Department of Tourism
Find links to Lithuanian tourism organizations, as well as customs and visa information, bank services and details about national holidays.

Tourism@Bude
Essential tourism guide celebrating the natural wonders and "must see" attractions of this coastal region. Displays events, photos and lodgings.

Tourism in Cheshire
The Cheshire County Council plays host to this concise tourism presentation. Displays local facts, attractions and lodging options.

Tourism in Paris
Guide to Paris attractions is mostly in French but offers some information in English. Learn about museums, transportation and activities.

MerseyWorld – Liverpool Tourism
Tourism section of the MerseyWorld site provides info and links for virtual tours, visitor centres, transport, attractions and accommodations.

West Sussex Tourism
Enjoy a variety of must see attractions, historic landmarks and popular leisure activities concerning the West Sussex region.

Strasbourg Tourism Office
Provides a guide to a variety of tourism options such as museums, hotels, attractions and restaurants.

Alsace Tourism
Learn about seasonal activities and festivals, and find links to Alsatian businesses. Also posts maps and pictures.

Figure 2.12 Search results from LookSmart.

If you prefer browsing by category to running keyword searches, LookSmart offers an 'Explore' mode that makes this easy. Click a major category from the list at the left of the page and a list of subcategories will appear beside it. Click a subcategory to see a third level of categories, and so on. After a few clicks, a page of links to sites related to a specific category will open.

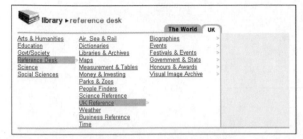

Figure 2.13 Moving through subject categories using LookSmart's 'Explore' mode.

UK-specific search engines

This section takes a look around search engines specifically built to provide links to sites in the UK. If you know that the information you want can only be found on a UK site, these search engines make an excellent starting point.

UK Plus
http://www.ukplus.co.uk
UK Plus is a category-based directory site, in a similar vein to Yahoo!. Its great strength is that every site listed has been reviewed by the folk at UK Plus. As this is obviously a time-consuming business, UK Plus is a good deal smaller than traditional robot-built search databases. However, the immediate benefit is that you have a good idea of what a site will contain before you click the link to visit it. Robot-built databases pick up the bad sites with the good, and what you find when you arrive at one of those sites may differ enormously from what the site's description led you to expect!

Figure 2.14 The UK Plus logo.

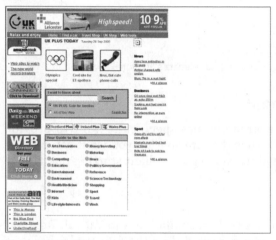

Figure 2.15 The simple search form and category list at UK Plus.

As with Yahoo! and LookSmart, you can search the directory by selecting a major category from the UK Plus home page and drilling down to more specific subcategories. For a faster automated search, use the text field and buttons at the top of the home page. You can also run an Infoseek-powered search of the entire Web by clicking the radio button marked 'all of the Web'.

There are two extra interesting points to note about UK Plus. First, you can link directly to Scotland Plus, Wales Plus and Ireland Plus by clicking small logos on the front page. These essentially lead to subsets of the main UK Plus site, but if you're looking for information that's specifically Welsh, for instance, this type of option could help you find it a lot faster. Second, UK Plus doesn't restrict itself to UK sites alone. The focus is on the *UK user* and what he or she will find useful, so you will find some American and international sites through UK Plus.

Yell.com
http://www.yell.com
We're not allowed to say that Yell.com is the online incarnation of the Yellow Pages directory, but we can say that it's a powerful search site owned by British Telecom that allows you to find businesses and companies anywhere in the UK from a simple keyword search. You'll find a range of useful services at Yell.com:

Figure 2.16 Searching for business at Yell.com.

- Cinema: pick a region, select one or more towns and/or type in a film title to find out what's showing at your local cinema.
- Property: a variety of property-related services such as estate agents, surveyors and removal firms, along with an invaluable Neighbourhood Information section.
- Travel: for all things travel-related, including airlines, accommodation, ferry services, and a currency converter.
- Weather: five-day weather forecasts for anywhere in the world.
- Shopping: over a dozen categories of online store to choose from, and growing.

Figure 2.17 A typical set of search results from Yell.com.

Searching for businesses couldn't be easier. At the top of most pages at Yell.com you'll see a yellow strip containing the search fields. Just enter a company name (if you're looking for a particular company) or a type of business, and select the location of the business. If the search engine doesn't recognise your choice of category name, a list of similar names will appear that you can choose from.

The search results list company names, addresses and telephone numbers, along with 'Map' links you can click to find your way on the ground. If the company has a Web site you can visit, you can click a 'Web Site' link to jump straight there.

Rampant Scotland Directory
http://www.rampantscotland.com

What it is that makes Scotland rampant isn't explained, but this comprehensive searchable directory an ideal starting point to find is Scottish sites and information. The large number of categories (and relatively small number of sites) means that a few clicks on the category titles should quickly lead you to what you want. If you prefer, you can run a keyword search of Rampant Scotland, or a metasearch of the entire Web (see Chapter 4) to combine hits from five major international search engines.

UK Index
http://www.ukindex.co.uk

These days many search sites are becoming **portals** – complete Web guides offering links to shopping, finance, news and weather, sport, you name it. The benefit of a portal is that you can start your everyday surfing at your favourite portal and use it as a launchpad to whatever you fancy doing. But if all you want to do is run a quick keyword search (one that isn't going to involve Boolean operators and advanced search options), you'd probably much rather just see a search field and a button! Its simplicity is one area where UK Index wins.

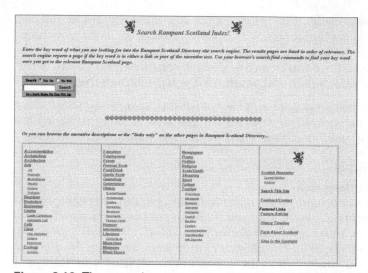

Figure 2.18 The comprehensive category list and simple search form at Rampant Scotland.

Being simple doesn't make UK Index useful by itself, of course. Its unique feature is a set of icons placed beside links in the search results. These icons show the date that the link was last checked by UK Index and what the result of that check was: if a range of sites was found, you can save yourself time by initially ignoring any sites that were noted as 'Not Found', 'Gone', or 'Timed Out' and heading straight for sites with a green tick beside them.

Figure 2.19 Icons in UK Index search results provide extra useful information.

Mirago
http://www.mirago.co.uk
http://www.mirago.co.uk/zone
The Mirago search engine has several features that recommend it, but one in particular stands out: clicking the link marked **Family Friendly** in the upper-left corner will take you to the second of the URLs above – a 'safe' version of the search engine. This option uses a combination of automatic and manual filtering to remove links and site descriptions that you wouldn't want your kids

to see (and you might not want to see them yourself, for that matter). While these filters are not entirely infallible, they do give a good reason for adding the 'safe' version of this site to your browser's Favorites or Bookmarks lists.

The search options themselves are equally comprehensive on either version of the site, allowing you to search for UK sites, or sites containing images, sounds, video or multimedia. Simple Boolean operators can be selected from the drop-down 'Look For' box:

- all of the words;
- any of the words;
- a person's name;
- words as a phrase;
- words near each other in the document;
- resources using Boolean operators.

Selecting the last of those options allows you to use advanced syntax to refine your search. The operators AND, OR, NOT and NEAR can be used, and phrases can be specified by enclosing them between double quotes.

You can also enclose expressions in brackets, as with Excite, and add an asterisk wildcard to the end of a word (for example, a search for 'south*' would return hits on 'southern' and 'Southampton').

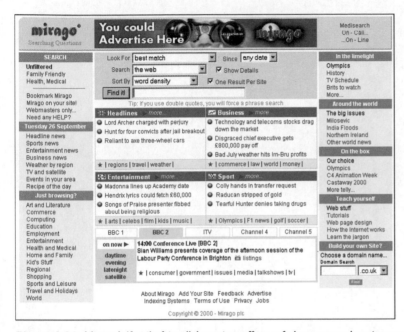

Figure 2.20 Mirago's 'family-friendly' version offers safe but comprehensive searching.

Worldwide search engines

3

Worldwide search engines

Which search engine is best?

Worldwide search engines

These are the giants of the world of search engines, being both the oldest and the largest. Most of them catalogue millions of Web pages. This is what we want, of course, but it can also cause problems: with millions of pages indexed, a search could easily yield several-hundred-thousand hits! Therefore you need to make your request specific using advanced search functions which allow you to combine particular terms and to filter the results.

AltaVista
http://www.altavista.com
The search engine of the computer manufacturer Digital Equipment is one of the leaders on the Internet. A number of search tools, including Yahoo! and Bigfoot, also use AltaVista technology. This was developed in the research laboratories of Digital Equipment at Palo Alto. It was in 1995 that AltaVista first appeared on the Web, with the ambition of cataloguing the entire Internet! A catalogue which represents around 200 Gb in its global version, and which will be polled in less than one second in most cases!

AltaVista offers a global search of the Web or Usenet (newsgroups). It is possible to search in the language of your choice. By default, the search engine is set to Any language. It is possible to indicate your preferences to the search engine, enabling you to save time.

The Advanced search mechanism will be used when, for example, it is necessary to use Boolean expressions or a document validity range (dates).

In normal search mode, AltaVista sorts hits by order of relevance. This mechanism is no longer active in Advanced search mode. It is up to you to activate it if necessary, using the Ranking text box, otherwise hits will be shown in random order.

You can carry out textual searches using inverted commas to quote phrases. You can also run more specific searches using the range of functions mentioned in Chapter 2, such as:

Domain. Search in a particular domain (.com, .org, .fr, etc.).

Image. Search for photographs, for example.

Link. Search for links.

AltaVista also allows you to search for images, audio and video files, maps and directions, people, products and companies. Through its BabelFish translator (**http://babel.altavista.com/translate.dyn**) it can also translate free text or entire Web pages. AltaVista offers a 'family-friendly' option which filters descriptions and links relating to adult sites: click the link labelled **Family Filter is Off** to find out more about this option.

Figure 3.1 The main search box of AltaVista.

Searching by date
It is possible to filter hits based on the date of documents. To do this you must complete the FROM and TO text boxes. Dates must be completed in the dd/mmm/yy format, where dd and yy represent days and years and mmm represents the first three letters of the month.

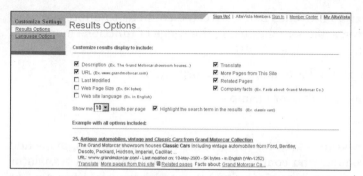

Figure 3.2 Choose how AltaVista's results should be presented.

Along with its Advanced mode, mentioned earlier, AltaVista offers a Power Search mode which is also available from its front page. Rather than constructing your own advanced search query using Boolean operators, you can select the options you want from drop-down lists and checkboxes.

Since July 1997, AltaVista has offered searching in 25 different languages. It uses a multilingual dictionary to determine the dominant language of each page indexed. It is therefore possible to display the hits corresponding to the language of your choice. This is much more efficient than searching by domain.

Excite
http://www.excite.com/
Another giant, since Excite updates an index of 50 million Web addresses (URLs). This search engine is very powerful, offers searching by category and keyword, and produces hits in order of relevance.

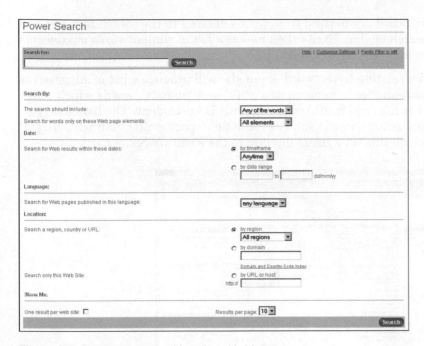

Figure 3.3 Run a 'power search' easily at AltaVista.

Excite is original in more than one way and has a very useful function called *Excite Search Wizard*. At the end of a search, the Wizard suggests a list of words that you can then add to another search. To do this, just check one or more words in the list of suggestions.

The words proposed are derived from words entered in the search text box and sent to the search engine. Excite then makes a list of similar words or concepts to help you to express your requests.

Thus, a search relating to the word 'kennedy' will produce a list of suggestions including 'assassination', 'assassinated', 'jfk' and 'onassis', words which make reference to the life (and death) of the famous US president. The list of suggestions will also include words such as 'shuttle' (space craft), 'launch', 'flight' and 'nasa', which this time relate directly to the *Kennedy Space Center*.

Figure 3.4 The Excite home page.

Take note of Excite's suggestions; they can be of real assistance in formulating your requests.

This highly practical mechanism is not yet available in Power Search, but will be in the future. In the meantime, it is quite sufficient to use it in normal search mode.

Excite also offers specialist services such as:

■ searching for maps and directions;

Figure 3.5 The result of searching with Excite.

■ searching for people (People Finder);

■ searching for companies in the United States (Yellow Pages).

Yahoo!
http://www.yahoo.com/
Here is another heavyweight search engine. More of a guide-directory than a traditional search engine, Yahoo! operates according to the same general principles for the user. It sends categories and sites corresponding to the request.

Yahoo! also offers a current events search service: News Articles and Net Events.

Yahoo! searches in four directions (or four databases):

■ **Yahoo! Categories.** The categories and subcategories constituting the highly detailed classification of the search guide.

■ **Yahoo! Web Sites.** Web sites in the strict sense.

■ **Yahoo!'s Net Events & Chat.** Live events and chat.

■ **Most Recent News Articles.** Current events items.

Yahoo! sends any categories found that match your search query, then a list of matching sites from Yahoo!'s own catalogue. If no matches are found, Yahoo! then runs a full search on the Web using the Google search engine (**http://www.google.com**) for the job.

Yahoo! evaluates the results of a request according to three main rules:

■ documents containing the most keywords are the most relevant;

■ documents whose titles contain keywords take priority over those where the words searched for appear only in the body of the Web page or in its address;

- the most general categories (at the top of Yahoo!'s Internet hierarchy) are better ranked than more specific categories (which are therefore at the bottom of the hierarchy).

Yahoo! also offers all sorts of additional services, such as:

- searching for people;
- searching for maps;
- searching for companies.

And also more original services such as:

- Yahoo! Shopping. A search tool for online shopping at **http:// shopping.yahoo.com**.
- Yahooligans! A search engine dedicated to sites for (and by) children, at **http:// www.yahooligans.com**.

Figure 3.6 Searching with Yahoo!

HotBot
http://www.hotbot.com
Created by the famous American magazine *Wired*, and owned by the giant Lycos search network, HotBot also plays in the court of the large search engines.

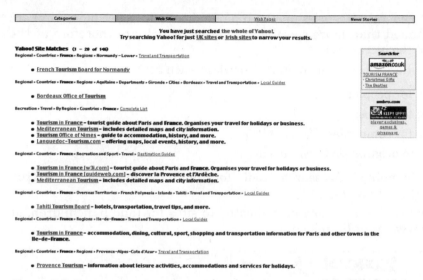

Figure 3.7 Presentation of results – categories and sites.

With HotBot, you are always running a semi-advanced search. The controls at the left of the page are set at default values, so you can ignore them, type a word or phrase into the text field and click the **Search** button. But you can also easily change options from this panel on the left:

- The language to search for
- The way the keywords are interpreted (as an exact phrase, separate phrases, a person's name, a Boolean expression, and so on)

Figure 3.8 A search tool for sites for children.

■ The date the information appeared on the Web

■ Content on the page (images, videos, MP3 audio and JavaScript)

You can also choose how many hits should appear on each page of results, and how detailed the information should be.

Figure 3.9 Searching with HotBot.

If you find yourself setting up the same combination of search options every time you come here, you can save yourself the bother: click the **Personalize These Settings** button, and a long form allows you to set up your search options the way you'd like to see them each time you arrive at HotBot.

The HotBot search engine also allows other searches:

- Directories of email addresses
- White Pages (searching for people)
- Yellow Pages (searching for businesses)

Figure 3.10 Searching for current news headlines at HotBot.

Figure 3.11 Searching for e-mail addresses using HotBot.

- News headlines and stock quotes
- Discussion groups

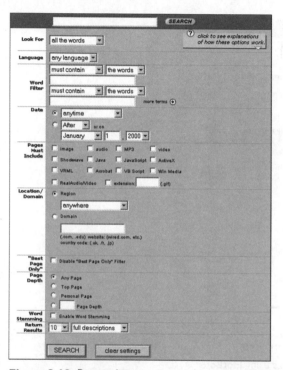

Figure 3.12 Personalising your search options at HotBot.

- FTP search for files (see Chapter 6)
- Music files and sites

HotBot offers a comprehensive set of features when you click the **Advanced Search** link. On the detailed form that appears, you can enter:

- additional words or phrases;
- the date or validity range for pages;
- where to search (a region, continent, Web site, domain or country code);
- how to return the search results;
- the media to be found on pages (images, sounds, animations, etc.). You can even state the type of file searched for by indicating the extension!

Ask Jeeves
http://www.ask.com
Although the precise details can vary from one engine to another, you have probably realised that the majority of search engines offer some method of constructing 'advanced' searches. Here's a search engine that takes things a long way in the opposite direction: you just roll up to the Ask Jeeves Web site and

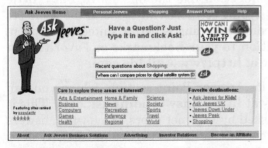

Figure 3.13 Ask Jeeves a question at this refreshingly simple search site.

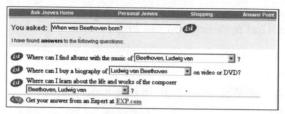

Figure 3.14 Pick the question that most closely matches what you were asking and click the Ask button to find the answer.

type a question like *When was Beethoven born?* This is known as 'natural language' searching. It isn't as effective as a well-constructed Boolean query at AltaVista, but it isn't trying to be.

Ask Jeeves works by identifying the key words in your question, and stripping out the rest. It then consults a list of questions containing the same key words to which it knows the answer and presents those to you to choose from. It's a comfortable feeling to type a 'real' question like the one above, but a little experimentation reveals that simply typing *beethoven* will lead to the same set of responses. The Ask Jeeves method of searching is better suited to children, and if you're a parent a good addition to your Bookmarks or Favorites list would be the Ask Jeeves For Kids site at **http://www.ajkids.com**.

One great bonus of Ask Jeeves is its Answer Point section, which you can reach from the main page or directly at **http://answerpoint.ask.com**. This is an excellent database of questions asked by Internet users, some with answers and some without. You can search this database, or a particular category of it, submit a question which will (with luck) be answered by another surfer, or browse around and add an answer to any question which hasn't yet been answered (or to which you can add some extra information).

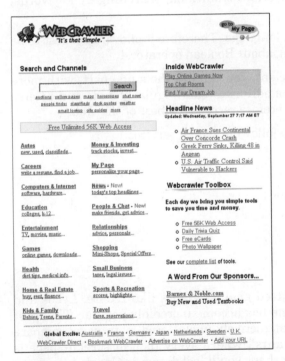

Figure 3.15 The WebCrawler home page.

WebCrawler
http://webcrawler.com/

WebCrawler is a subsidiary trademark of Excite, so may not have a long-term future. However, it exists, and it offers traditional searching by keywords, which gives good results.

WebCrawler also works in natural language. Therefore it allows a request to be expressed simply, without worrying about Boolean operators!

If the search function is not sufficient, you can use the guide part, with more than 5,000 sites per category. The editorial team regularly adds and deletes sites from this catalogue, which therefore records the best of the Web.

In addition, WebCrawler offers the following search services:

- yellow pages;
- newsgroups;
- searching for people (see Chapter 5);
- maps;
- classified ads.

Google
http://www.google.com

Appearing from nowhere, and pitted against giants like Excite, Lycos and AltaVista, the Google search engine has become incredibly popular. The most likely reason for its success is its attractively uncluttered main page: compare this to the front pages of the 'giants', where every inch of screen-space is trying to get your attention, and perhaps you'll feel drawn to Google too.

Not that you can't run an advanced search here, though. Click the **Advanced Search** link above the text field and you'll be moved to a page containing a convenient set of text fields and drop-down lists allowing you to search for:

- Words or a phrases that must be included or excluded
- Domains to include or exclude
- Pages in particular languages
- Pages that link to, or are similar to, a certain page

You can also set up a range of preferences relating to language and the display of search results; these preferences can be saved so that they'll be automatically applied each time you use Google. Best of all, Google offers a SafeSearch feature that aims to filter 'adult' content out of the search results, and this option is also stored with your other preferences.

Figure 3.16 The refreshingly simple Google page.

Go.com
http://www.go.com

This engine was formerly known as InfoSeek, and you can still reach the UK version of the engine at **http://www.infoseek.co.uk**, as mentioned in Chapter 2. Along with the catchier name, Go.com has grown a few new features (although it pays to remember that as an 'international' search engine, the majority of these will be aimed mostly at American users):

- Search for people (white pages)
- Search for maps and driving directions
- Search for businesses (yellow pages)
- Use an online dictionary or translation service

When running a search from the front page of the site, you can choose between searching for Web pages, for images, or for audio and video files. If you prefer, you can delve Yahoo!-style into a comprehensive set of directory categories. Advanced searching happens on a separate page reached by clicking the **Search Options** link below the search field, and you can construct searches using an easy-to-use but powerful set of form controls which allow you to search in page titles, URLs and hyperlinks as well as entire documents. You can opt to show results only from a particular domain, or exclude a domain. Finally, you can choose to confine your search to particular topic categories and/or to certain countries.

While you're on the Search Options page, you can also choose different types of search, such as stocks, newsgroups, shareware and general reference.

As an extra bonus (something that more and more search engines are adding), Go.com offers Goguardian, an option to filter out inappropriate content from

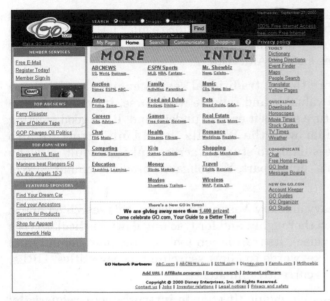

Figure 3.17 The Go.com home page.

search results. This can optionally be password controlled, allowing you to bypass it when you need to.

Which search engine is best?

Needless to say, there isn't one search engine that's always better than all the others. The ideal search engine for one purpose may be too simplistic for another and overkill for a third. With experimentation, you'll probably settle on the two or three search engines you like best for regular use, that cover all bases: for example, a directory like Yahoo!, a simple search engine like Google, and a more powerful engine such as AltaVista.

Yahoo! is a directory more than a traditional search engine, but it's been around for years and is a valuable and reliable workhorse. Its range of categories and hierarchical nature makes it easy to understand. It's a good starting point for anyone unfamiliar with the Web. Its 'hand-built' structure also means that you are far less likely to stumble across links to 'adult' sites by accident here. Its children's counterpart, Yahooligans!, provides similar ease of use and safety for kids.

AltaVista is the Web's heavy artillery. Vast and powerful, this search engine is useful for scanning the Web thoroughly, and for tracking down particular types of file (images, audio and video). Its translation tool is sometimes helpful (and often amusing). Its set of keywords to allow searching in page titles, URLs, domain names, and so on, is currently unmatched.

Excite is an intelligent search engine. It tries to interpret your request (by comparing it to past searches by other users) and suggests similar words and concepts to help you refine your search. Excite tends to be less useful when searching for phrases than when searching for single words.

WebCrawler is Excite's directory site. It does things a little differently from Yahoo!, which you may like, and it has a useful Ask An Expert section of question-and-answer sites.

HotBot has a lot in common with AltaVista – to the point, perhaps, that the presence of the Advanced Search controls on HotBot's front page might be the deciding factor on which you prefer. Along with its ability to search a number of resources, HotBot can find pages based on type of content (images, video, scripts, and so on).

Ask Jeeves (and its children's counterpart, **Ask Jeeves For Kids**) are at the simple end of the spectrum. The layout and style is friendly, making this a great search engine for Internet beginners. The AnswerPoint area is useful and unique, and worth remembering whether or not you use the search engine itself.

Google is deceptively simple. Its popularity lies in its uncluttered interface, but advanced options and 'family-friendly' searching are available if you need them.

Go.com is the closest match to Yahoo!, offering a well-constructed directory alongside keyword searching. It's also one of the best sites to search for people (e-mail addresses, phone numbers, and so on).

Metasearch engines

4

Metasearch engines

Collections of search engines and directories

Experienced surfers all have their favourite search engine. Some swear by AltaVista, while others prefer Yahoo! or maybe UK Plus for searching UK sites. To search for information there is another solution: metasearch engines. Their principle is simple: you indicate the keywords corresponding to your request and the metasearch engine sends the request to the various search engines.

Another possibility is to use search engine groupings on the same page. This facilitates intensive searching and allows you to have a list of powerful tools to hand.

Metasearch engines

They use the power of several search engines without you having to worry about it. They differ in terms of the choice of search engine and the evaluation of the results given to you.

CNET Search.com
http://www.search.com
This easy-to-remember URL takes you to a site that was formerly known as Savvy Search, but has now become part of the massive CNET Networks organisation.

A metasearch engine, Search.com gives you the fastest replies in searching Yahoo!, Lycos, GoTo.Com, Inktomi and Direct Hit, along with 700 smaller and specialised search engines.

To start the search, type the keywords and click the search button. You can refine your search using double-quotes to denote phrases, + and – symbols to include or exclude a particular word or phrase, and the Boolean operators **and**, **or** and **not**. Using a standard search, only a small number of search engines

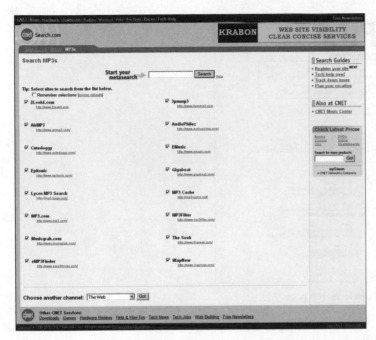

Figure 4.1 A search for MP3 audio at Search.com involves up to 16 different search engines!

are polled. By clicking a category from the directory-structure below, however, you'll be taken to a page from which you can search a collection of engines that specialise in the topic you chose.

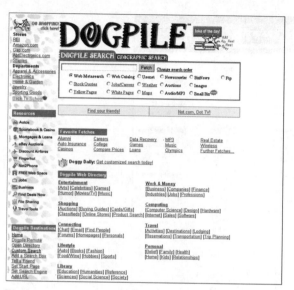

Figure 4.2 The main Dogpile search page.

Dogpile
http://www.dogpile.com

This powerful metasearch engine can target 10 areas of the Internet for searching. Most usefully, of course, Dogpile searches the Web, presenting search results from 14 popular engines quickly and effectively. By selecting the appropriate radio button you can also search Usenet (newsgroup) archives, FTP servers, world and business news headlines or stock quotes.

Being a US site, the remaining options on Dogpile's main page are not espe-
cially useful to the UK user. You'll rarely need to search for businesses, people,
maps or weather forecasts in the US. But a click on the International link at
the top of the page will take you to a list of similar services covering a number
of other countries. The UK is particularly well served here, with search options
including Business Finder, People Finder, Local Information and Travel Guide.

InFind
http://www.infind.com
InFind is not simply a point of access to the various search engines. It can combine the searches carried out by the different search engines and return a
single list to you after deleting redundancies.

InFind polls the best search engines on the Web: Yahoo!, Lycos, AltaVista,
Infoseek, Excite and WebCrawler. Each search engine is active in parallel. If
one search engine gathers 300 results at once, whereas its neighbour only

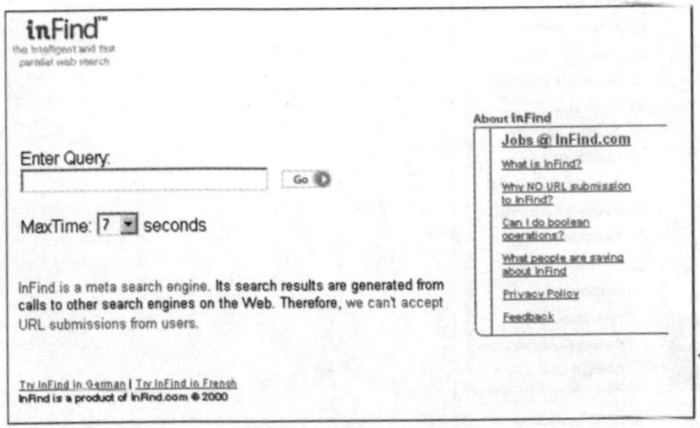

Figure 4.3 Searching with InFind.

gathers 10, the latter will be polled 30 more times. With InFind, search engines work flat out! Then all the results from the six sources are analysed. Redundancies and similar documents are eliminated in order to produce the most appropriate list of results.

It is impossible to carry out manually what InFind provides automatically, so why go without?

The search time can be limited, which is very often useful. Results are displayed by heading and include a list of titles only, each title giving access to the corresponding site.

Mamma
http://www.mamma.com

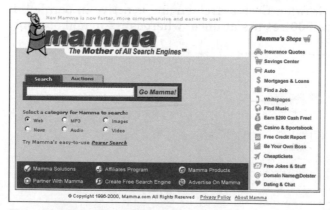

Figure 4.4 Welcome to Mamma!

Mamma is there to take care of you and will put your request to 10 well-known search engines, including:

- AltaVista;
- Excite;
- Infoseek;
- Lycos;
- WebCrawler;
- Yahoo!.

Not forgetting DejaNews for searching newsgroups (see Chapter 6).

Select the search domain, check the appropriate option boxes (activation of summaries, searches based on a phrase, searches based on page titles) and click on **Search**. Mamma will do the rest for you.

Meta Crawler
http://www.metacrawler.com
This is one of the veteran metasearch engines and uses several search engines to meet your requirements. Created in 1995 at Washington University, Meta Crawler was bought by the go2net company in 1997.

Also worth discovering is Mini Crawler in which a small window is opened on the screen. This is highly practical as it means that you can have a metasearch engine on standby in a corner of your Windows Office to search the Web at any moment.

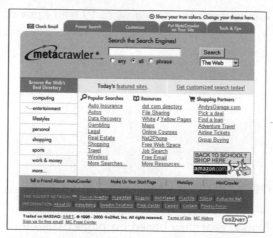

Figure 4.5 Meta Crawler at your service!

Figure 4.6 The Mini Crawler window.

Copernic
http://www.copernic.com

Copernic isn't exactly a search engine in the way we've come to think of them – it isn't a Web site, for one thing, it's a software program. Visit the Copernic site to download and install one of the family of search tools available, and you can simply start this program whenever you want to run a metasearch. Over 80 engines can be searched, and you can confine your search to particular categories of engine.

Because Copernic is a program running on your own computer, you can create and save advanced searches for reuse in the future. Just click any of the search results to go to that site in your default browser.

Figure 4.7 The results of metasearching the Web using Copernic

Collections of search engines and directories

These compilations of the best tools are practical for carrying out intensive searches and comparing the results of several search engines.

The Internet Sleuth
http://www.isleuth.com/
This is a fantastic tool which gives access to more than 2,000 databases.

The original feature of the site is that it only catalogues sites having a search text box. The site search mechanism is displayed on Sleuth according to the requests made. Searches are carried out by subject and not by specific request. Do not ask for the recipe for duck à l'orange, since no database is concerned with this. Search for the word 'recipe' instead. You will then have access to databases relating to cooking.

You thus obtain a list of hits, each entry point having its own search text box and that of the database corresponding to the initial search. At this stage you can search for the recipe for duck à l'orange in the databases proposed. Sleuth therefore allows you to search for and find everything worth searching for … and finding!

Six specific domains are offered:

- search engines;
- directory sites;
- news;
- business and finance;
- software;
- Usenet (newsgroups).

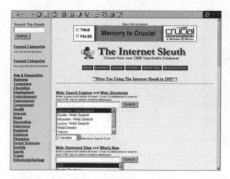

Figure 4.8 The home page of Internet Sleuth.

Figure 4.9 Searching in compilations of sites.

The method is the same for all six categories. Enter the keywords, select the search engine or site and click on the **Search** button.

On the left of the home page you can select a subject or sub-subject of interest. You can also indicate a maximum search time in order not to tie up your PC unnecessarily. By default, the value is fixed at two minutes.

Search engines to search for search engines!

You can use a search engine such as Yahoo! to search for other search engines. Go directly to the following address: **http://dir.yahoo.com/ Computers_and_ Internet/Internet/World _WideWeb/Searching_ the_Web**

Yahoo! offers the following tools in particular:

- *195 search engines!*

- *109 metasearch engines or search engine grouping pages!*

- *211 Web directories!*

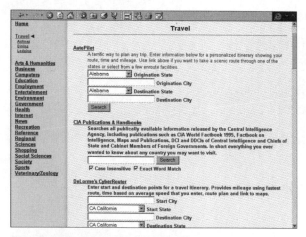

Figure 4.10 An extract from the 'Travel' selection page.

Aztech Cyberspace Launch Pad
http://www.aztech-cs.com/aztech/surf_central.html

This site offers a simple list of search engines and the possibility of searching directly from this page.

Directory Guide
http://www.directoryguide.com/

This service is a compilation of search tools, directories and guides – 400 of these have been referenced and are accessible by keywords.

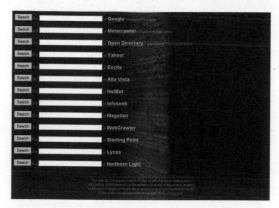

Figure 4.11 The choice of a metasearch engine or one of the large international search engines on the home page.

Web Taxi
http://www.webtaxi.com/

Select an international search engine, a regional search engine (by country throughout the world) or a subject, and click on the **Search** button. Web Taxi then displays the tool or tools found at the bottom of the screen. The rest is up to you.

Directories of people and companies

Finding people and e-mail addresses

Trademarks and companies

The Yellow Pages

Apart from the vast source of information and services which the Web constitutes, the Internet is also a means of communication. E-mail is the most frequently used application, just in front of the Web. Contacting others and finding a company are the frequent needs of surfers.

Searches for people may be based on addresses, telephone numbers or e-mail addresses. There are specialist tools and services on the Web for each of these requirements. We have already seen that most large search engines (see Chapters 2 and 3) offer search functions relating to people, e-mail addresses and Yellow Pages services. This chapter gives us the opportunity to introduce some new ones and to look at the most reliable ways of tracking down people and companies.

There are millions of us around the world who use the Internet to communicate. So, if you have lost somebody's details, if you are looking for somebody who has disappeared, if you wish to make contacts abroad, this is your opportunity.

Finding people and e-mail addresses

Some tools specialise in searching individual countries; others search the whole planet unless you choose to restrict searching to a particular country. However, in the UK (as in many other countries), finding people is by no means an exact science – there are no directories relating exclusively to UK residents. We'll begin by looking at the worldwide services most likely to lead you to an Internet user in the UK. Remember that you can actually use these services to find someone anywhere in the world simply by selecting the appropriate country.

In the UK

InfoSpace Email Addresses
http://www.infospace.com/info/email1.htm

By default, the InfoSpace Email Addresses lookup offers a search of 'Any Country', so your first step must be to select 'United Kingdom' from the list of countries. Enter the last and first name of the person you want to find and, optionally, their home town or city. Ignore the State/Province box which relates only to American searches, and click the **Find Email** button.

Figure 5.1 Starting an e-mail address search at InfoSpace.

InfoSpace has various methods of gathering its information, so the details available for each person in the results list will vary. If the person is registered with InfoSpace, you may find their address, phone number and more when you click on their name. InfoSpace doesn't display the e-mail address, but provides a link you can click to send an e-mail message.

Figure 5.2 The result of searching at InfoSpace.

InfoSpace Phone Numbers
http://www.infospace.com/info/people.htm

Along with the e-mail address search mentioned above, InfoSpace also makes a great job of finding someone's postal address and telephone number. The form is almost identical to the e-mail addresses lookup, but there's one difference to note when completing the fields: unless the person you are searching for has an unusual name, try to enter the town or city as well as the country. If you don't, the service may return hundreds of matches!

Figure 5.3 InfoSpace is the best place to find a UK resident's address and phone number.

Throughout the world

Yahoo! People Search
http://people.yahoo.com
This site has replaced one of the old stalwarts, Four11 (in fact the URL **www.four11.com** will still get you here), but it's still one of the best places to find an e-mail address. All the same, the fact that your correspondent has an e-mail address does not necessarily mean that you will find it. There is no shortage of addresses! For example, it is not easy to know which is the right Bill Gates from among the 70 found! Is just one of them the boss of Microsoft? By clicking on the headers listed, you obtain more specific information and can then proceed by elimination.

WhoWhere?
http://www.whowhere.lycos.com/
WhoWhere? is a well-known US search service, part of the Lycos network of search engines. The service delivers highly detailed results which may include the address, phone number and hobbies of people who have registered with the service.

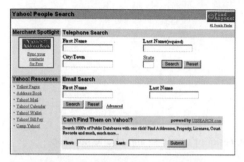

Figure 5.4 The Yahoo! People Search home page.

The WhoWhere? search engine works by approximation. The search criterion does not need to correspond to an exact entry in the index. Therefore typing or spelling errors in entering names are not too much of a problem. The search engine will in fact find overlaps of strings of two characters or more. It even allows searches using initials!

The service also offers:

- searching for addresses and telephone numbers;
- searching for companies on the Internet;
- Yellow Pages: all companies (not necessarily present on the Net). Note the Big Book service for finding companies in the United States.

Bigfoot
http://www.bigfoot.com
The service offers:

Figure 5.5 Details of contacts found, with e-mail addresses and links to more information.

- searching for e-mail addresses; or
- the white pages (people's addresses).

In addition to the service, Bigfoot indicates how it has obtained the information. This may be useful in making an unsuccessful search more specific.

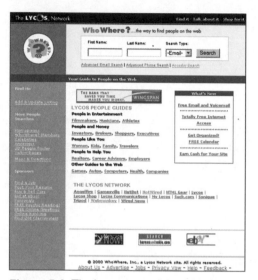

Figure 5.6 The home page of the WhoWhere? service.

At Bigfoot, listed users may remain anonymous if they wish. In simple terms, you can find them, even send them an e-mail, but without knowing their address (this remains hidden).

AOL NetFind
http://www.aol.com/netfind/whitepages.adp
America Online is well-known as an online service offering private content to its members, but AOL also includes a useful range of services at its Web site

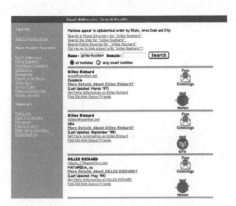

Figure 5.7 Search results are presented in order of relevance (Highly, Probably or Possibly Relevant).

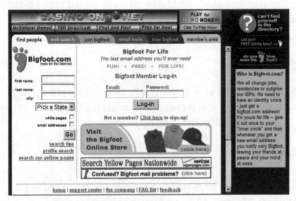

Figure 5.8 The Bigfoot home page.

Collections of search engines

If the search engines mentioned previously are not enough, or if you want to access them from the same page, use one of the All In One services for finding people and e-mail addresses, such as **http://www.allone-search.com/allluser.html#People**. *Dozens of e-mail address search engines are thus accessible, in alphabetical order, from 411 Locate to Yahoo! People Search.*

The same service is provided on The Front Page (**http://www.thefront-page.com/search**)

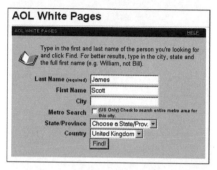

Figure 5.9 Searching for a person.

(**www.aol.com**). The White Pages section of AOL NetFind is actually provided by InfoSpace, mentioned earlier in this chapter, so there are no surprises in its people lookup, but from this page you can jump to international white pages directories or search through AOL's own users.

Trademarks and companies

Directories of trademarks and companies are legion on the Net. Here is a useful selection. You will need to distinguish between tools which only list companies present on the Web, and the others, of more general scope.

The Patent Office – Database Search
http://gb.espacenet.com
The Patent Office deals with UK trademark and patent applications. While the main site at **http://www.patent.gov.uk** provides useful background informa-

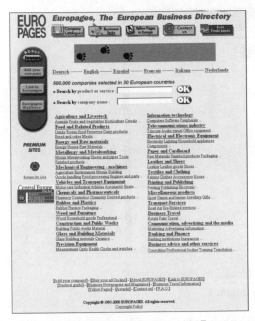

Figure 5.10 Finding companies using Europages.

continued

where you can select the People & Business options from the home page menu.
Are you looking for a telephone or fax number, an address or e-mail address **anywhere in the world?** Use Telephone Directories on the Web (**http://www.teldir.com/eng**). The directories of 44 countries are easily accessible. The service is quite austere, but highly efficient.

tion, the Database Search site allows you to search patent databases in the UK, Europe and worldwide.

Europages
http://www.europages.com/

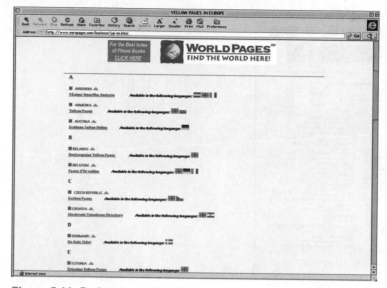

Figure 5.11 Finding directories of companies by country.

This European directory lists 500,000 companies spread over 30 countries in Europe.

You can search in three ways:

- in plain text mode;
- by business; or
- by company name.

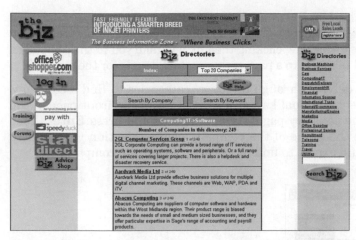

Figure 5.12 Categories, search form and company listings at The Business Information Zone.

Note the Yellow Pages button (**http://www.europages.com/business/yp-en.html**) which allows you to search through 17 European countries. Select the country and one of the languages offered (by clicking on the flag).

You then access a directory of companies for the country selected. Europages thus gives you easy access to the best company directories throughout Europe.

The Business Information Zone (the Biz)
http://www.thebiz.co.uk
This site provides one of the simplest ways to locate a UK company, whether the company you are searching for is present on the Internet or not. Using a directory

structure similar to the UK Plus and Yahoo! Web search engines, you work through categories and subcategories until you find the company you are looking for. If that company has a Web site, clicking the link will take you to the company's site. If not, the link will take you to a page giving contact details for the company.

If you're not keen on delving through directory categories to find a company, The Biz also offers the traditional keyword search. From the front page of the site, or from any of the category pages, type keywords and press **Enter**. Your keywords can include the name of the company or organisation you want to find, or words you would expect to find in a description of the company.

Figure 5.13 Search for US companies by name, industry or directory category.

CompaniesOnline
http://www.companiesonline.com

This is yet another service that forms a part of the huge Lycos network, and can provide detailed information about a large number of US companies. Along with contact details this information may include annual turnover, number of employees, the latest stock quote and much more.

Like The Biz, CompaniesOnline lets you choose between running a traditional search or 'drilling down' through category listings.

LookHere Web directory
http://www.lookhere.co.uk

If you know that the UK company you're looking for has a presence on the Web, LookHere may be able to take you to its site. LookHere's categories are organised by initial letter, so clicking 'C' on the home page will lead to a list of categories that includes Cars, Cinema and Construction. Click a category to see a page of links to companies in that category, accompanied by brief descriptions.

The Yellow Pages

The expression 'Yellow Pages' is widely used on the Web. These search sites allow you to find details of businesses and companies on the Internet.

With the formidable development of companies on the Web, there are plenty of Yellow Pages services. The large search engines have them, as we have already seen.

Yell
http://www.yell.com

Figure 5.14 Searching for businesses and companies at Yell.

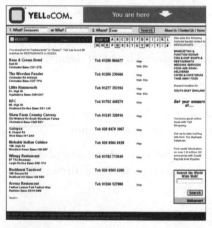

Figure 5.15 Yell's search results include clickable links to extra information.

Yell is the online incarnation of the UK Yellow Pages telephone directory. Its great benefit is that it covers the entire country rather than limiting you to searching in your own telephone area. You can choose between two methods of searching. Either select a business type (such as Painters and Decorators or Airlines) or search for a specific company by name. In the **Where?** Box, type a town, city or country.

Along with the name, address and phone number of businesses matching your search criteria, links may be included to indicate that the business has its own Web site, or provide a map or additional information.

Scoot
http://www.scoot.co.uk

Figure 5.16 Search for a product using Scoot's Product Finder directory.

Scoot provides a similar set of services to Yell, allowing you to search for a type of business or a company name, selected from links to the right of the search form. A useful extra is the Product Finder page, which can help you find businesses that provide the particular product or service you're looking for.

Kompass
http://www.kompass.com
This is a monster which lists 1.5 million companies throughout the world, spread over 61 countries!

There are two search modes:

- product search; or
- company search.

Instead of a keyword search you can use the Guided Search option, which is actually an unusual name for the directory-structure of categories found on many search sites. One clever addition at Kompass is that if you select a particular country or continent from the listbox above before picking a category, only companies from the selected area will be shown in the categorised lists.

Infospace
http://www.infospace.com
Finding companies is at the heart of this service. But you can also find white pages, and search for online purchasing sites, small ads, maps, etc.

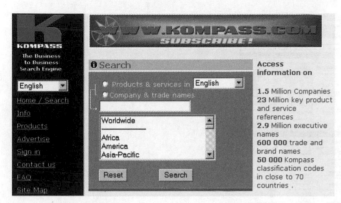

Figure 5.17 Welcome to the search for companies throughout the world.

Infospace offers several modes of operation for finding companies:

- by category;
- by name;
- by address, even if only approximate;
- by telephone or fax number;
- by map (US, Canada and London).

Figure 5.18 All the search tools accessible on Infospace.

Searching with Usenet and FTP

6

Newsgroups

Finding newsgroups on the Web

Finding download sites

Finding shareware

With the huge success of the Web, we have come to confuse the Web and the Internet. In fact, the Internet has a set of older resources such as:

- Usenet: for newsgroups or discussion groups;
- FTP (*File Transfer Protocol*): download sites.

These resources are increasingly accessible on the Web owing to their user-friendliness.

Newsgroups

Newsgroups are discussion groups covering particular subjects: HTML, languages, sciences, politics, humour, ketchup (yes, honestly!), and more. A *lot* more in fact: there are in excess of 50,000 different newsgroups in existence, although you may not be able to access all of them. Much depends upon which newsgroups your Internet service provider has chosen to subscribe to, but you will probably have a few tens of thousands available.

You can access newsgroups using a dedicated *newsreader* program such as Agent or Free Agent (**http://www.forteinc.com**), or TIFNY (**http://www.tifny2.com**), or you may be able to use features built into your e-mail program. For users of Internet Explorer 4 or later, the Outlook Express e-mail program makes it easy to work with newsgroups. Here we'll use Outlook Express, but the principles are the same with any other newsgroup program.

It pays to remember that among all the possible topics for newsgroups, sex and pornography are certainly included, along with other topics you may prefer not to encounter. Fortunately such groups are usually easy to spot by their names: you are less likely to stumble across pornographic newsgroups than Web sites.

Newsgroups are a great way of participating in life in cyberspace, communicating with others, and exchanging information. But, as with the Web, you need to find the right addresses!

Newsgroup addresses take the form *domain.subject.sub-subject*; e.g.: **alt.music.pop**.

Domains are represented by codes: **alt** for alternative, **comp** for newsgroups connected with computers, **rec** for recreational or **talk** for chatting and exchanging ideas.

Figure 6.1 Finding newsgroups using Outlook Express.

The All tab in the above figure provides a list of all the newsgroups accessible. The Subscribe tab contains a list of the newsgroups to which you have decided to subscribe.

Don't confuse newsgroups with chat rooms: newsgroup discussions don't take place in 'real time'. You read the messages posted, but you are not in direct communication with their authors. Likewise, when you post a message, this will be read by whoever wants to whenever they want. Interactive, or real time chatting, requires the IRC (or chat) technique, which we will deal with later.

Among the 50,000 or more newsgroups available, many will be 'worldwide' groups with contributors from anywhere in the world (although the dominant language is English, as elsewhere on the Internet). For some types of information search this wide range of contributors means you should be able to find what you want more quickly.

There may be times, however, when only UK-specific information will do: sifting through a worldwide newsgroup for UK legal advice would be a painful process! Fortunately there are a number of UK newsgroups covering a large number of subjects. These are easy to find since their names all begin with 'uk'.

Hundreds of newsgroups, sorted by alphabetical order, are directly accessible using your newsreader software. By typing a few letters in the text box above the list of groups, you access specific newsgroups faster. For example, type **uk** to go to the list of UK-specific newsgroups. Select a newsgroup and connect in order to consult it.

You will then learn:

- how to subscribe to a newsgroup;
- how to read messages off-line;
- how to participate in newsgroups by sending messages;
- how to find, organise and sort messages.

In fact, the enormous number of messages of some newsgroups makes them difficult to consult. However, search functions make it easy to access the information you want. You can carry out searches by indicating:

- the sender's name;
- a keyword or phrase to be matched in newsgroup messages;
- validity dates (posted before, or after).

Finding newsgroups on the Web

Once again, the Web is there to help you to find newsgroups. Some search engines offer this service, such as DejaNews, of which it is a speciality.

DejaNews
http://www.dejanews.com/
The correct URL is actually **http://www.deja.com**, since DejaNews has gone the way of many other search engines and started offering everything but the kitchen sink from its homepage. You then have to look for the option to search Usenet (the 'proper' name for newsgroups). Fortunately the **www.dejanews.com** URL still takes you straight to the part of the site you want.

Figure 6.2 The Deja.com logo, home of DejaNews.

When you arrive, it all looks very straightforward. Using the controls at the top of the page you can type keywords to search for, and choose whether to search only recent discussions, past discussions, or all discussions. From a second drop-down list you can choose to search in the following areas:

- Complete: all newsgroups
- Standard: all groups except those dealing with adult topics, jobs and small ads
- Adult: groups and messages dealing with 'adult' (usually pornographic) topics
- Jobs: groups and messages relating to job vacancies and recruitment
- For Sale: small ads, goods for sale, and so on

The 'Standard' option is selected by default, and that's usually the option you would want.

Figure 6.3 Search options at DejaNews.

Search results appear as a list of messages, much like e-mail messages in your Inbox. If a message's subject line seems to cover the topic you're interested in, click it to read the message. When the message is displayed, you can do a number of things:

- Switch to the previous or next message listed in the search results
- Compose a reply to the message
- Read a profile of the message's author (if a profile exists)
- Click the **Forum** link to switch to the group in which the message was found
- Click the **Thread** link to read the entire 'conversation' of which this message was a part

Also listed on the results page you'll find matches among newsgroup names. By checking boxes beside the appropriate names, you can re-run the search in those groups only to narrow the search. (An alternative is to start by searching

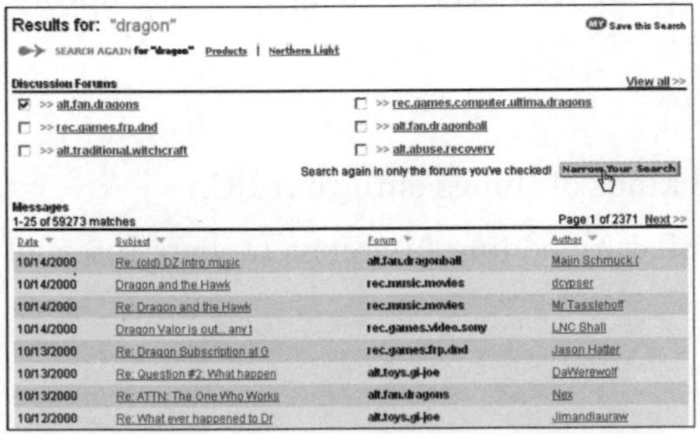

Figure 6.4 The results of a search at DejaNews.

No news?

If you can't find what you want at DejaNews, the chances are you won't find it in the newsgroups at all. DejaNews specialises in newsgroups and maintains a comprehensive database of groups and messages. Choosing the 'Search Usenet' (or equivalent) option at one of the search engines mentioned elsewhere in this book will usually result either in a search that uses DejaNews, or a search of the engine's own less comprehensive database.

for newsgroups by name: at the bottom of the main search page you'll see a second text box where you can search for groups rather than messages.)

Finally, DejaNews offers a comprehensive Power Search option. This has added power in that after setting up the search as you want it, it can be automatically applied to all your future searches. Options on the Power Search page include:

- Match: choose whether *all* words or *any* words should be regarded as a match (the equivalent of Boolean AND / OR searches)
- Forum: optionally choose which newsgroup to search in
- Author: restrict the search to messages from a particular author (by e-mail address)
- Dates: search for messages posted between specific dates
- Language: search for messages in a particular language

You can also choose whether search results should be sorted by confidence (how likely they are to be good matches for your search query), subject, author, newsgroup name, or date.

Finding download sites

Download sites are used to import all kinds of things onto your PC:

- programs, utilities and plug-ins (software adding functions to your Internet browser);
- shareware;
- drawings, images, photographs;
- sound files;

- videos;
- text documents.

The advantage of downloading software from a Web site rather than an FTP site is that it is simpler. Instead of going through directories, you let yourself be guided. And that avoids the need to use several different software programs.

FTP Search
http://ftpsearch.lycos.com
This Norwegian site, now operated by the Lycos Network, offers the option of searching FTP servers for files to download. Be warned: this service only works using file and directory names – there is no way to search by keyword (for exam-

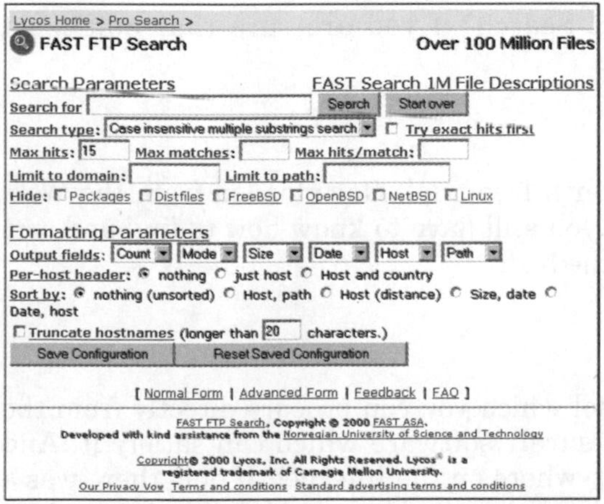

Figure 6.5 The FTP Search page (don't be put off – it really is easy!).

ple, searching for particular *types* of file). You must already know the name of the file you are looking for, or some part of the name. For example, if you want to find Windows screensavers, you might search for ***.scr** (which would find any files with the .scr extension). Or if you are trying to download a file called **newfile102.zip** from an FTP site but you're having trouble, you could find out whether that file exists on any other (perhaps more reliable!) FTP servers.

The search controls might look a bit daunting at first glance, but you can leave most of them at their defaults. Simply type the text you want to search for in the first text box and click **Search**. Other changes you might want to make are:

■ Increase **Max hits** from 15 to see more matching items per page
■ Check the **Try exact hits first box** if you are searching for a specific filename
■ Change **Search type** to 'Exact Search' if you are sure that non-exact matches will be of no use to you

Finding shareware

Shareware are programs which offer a free trial. Downloaded from the Web, they meet many requirements. But you still have to know how to find and sort the good, the very good even, from the bad!

Shareware.com
http://www.shareware.com
Shareware constitutes a valuable tool which you can procure directly from the Net. Whatever your need, there is surely software which can satisfy it. And shareware is to be found almost everywhere on the Internet. If only there was a site offering all existing shareware! Where you could get to know all the versions

and be sure of downloading the latest. Where you could also find products for Macs, PCs, computers that run under DOS, Windows 3.1 or 95 or even NT. One can dream... There would also need to be a short introduction to each software in order to know what it is used for and what its limits are. But wait, this service exists! It is called shareware.com.

From the homepage you can run a standard search (which involves typing the name or type of software you are looking for, and selecting the operating system you use), or an Advanced search. The Advanced search lets you choose from the following options:

- Search in the file's description
- Specify words that should not appear in the description
- Search in the file's name
- Specify the age of the file

You can choose whether to search by platform, or to select one or more software archives to search.

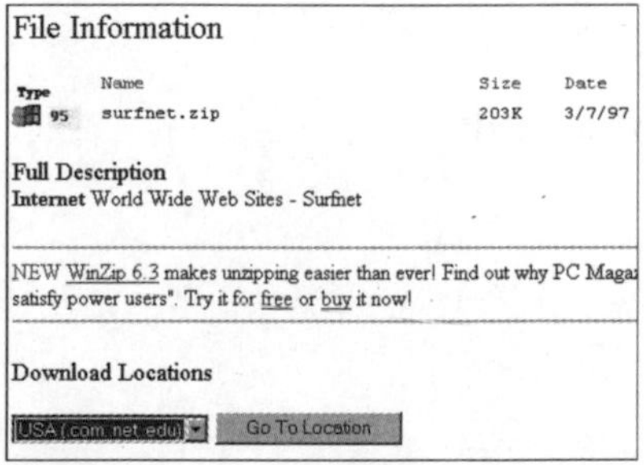

Figure 6.6 Finding software using Shareware.com.

Shareware – how to use it

Shareware is not free software. It is a program which you can try out free of charge. If the program suits you, and you wish to keep it, you must pay the author. The price of the licence and the programmer's details are generally mentioned in a 'readme.txt' file or are accessible when you start the product. Often, it is possible to register and pay for the product online. It is good to pay for the licence, it is one of the rules of the game. Moreover, you will then be able to benefit from upgrades or receive more detailed documentation. On the other hand, if the program does not meet your requirements, just delete it from your hard disk.

CNET · Shareware.com Search Results for screen saver		
Found: 500 Displaying: 1-25 <Previous 1 2 3 4 5 6 7 8 9 10 11 12 13 14 15 16 17 18 19 20 Next>		
Re-sort by Filename	Platform/Type	File Date
0a1image41.exe Display your images as screen savers - play music! **Location:** winsite-win95 archive **Directory:** desktop/ **Size:** 1.8MB	Windows 95	03/29/2000
0acreate1.exe Create and distribute Screen Savers with your images. **Location:** winsite-win95 archive **Directory:** desktop/ **Size:** 4.3MB	Windows 95	11/02/1999
0creata3.exe Create Screen Savers with your photos, images, graphics **Location:** winsite-win95 archive **Directory:** desktop/ **Size:** 1.8MB	Windows 95	03/24/1999
0s_ult56.zip SlideShow ULTRA - Incredible! Screen Saver JPG GIF BMP **Location:** winsite-win95 archive **Directory:** desktop/ **Size:** 3.5MB	Windows 95	10/20/1998
0void01.exe FreeWare Screen Saver featuring beautiful mountains **Location:** winsite-win95 archive **Directory:** desktop/ **Size:** 1MB	Windows 95	06/04/2000
0void02.exe Freeware Screen Saver featuring beautiful Ocean Scenes **Location:** winsite-win95 archive **Directory:** desktop/ **Size:** 825K	Windows 95	06/05/2000

Figure 6.7 The result of a search using the keywords 'screen saver'.

The results of a search reveal:

- the name of the file (the software) to be downloaded;
- a brief description of the program;
- the storage directory (category of program);
- the date of the file;
- the file size.

Figure 6.8 The Tucows homepage, with simple search controls at the top.

Tucows
http://tucows.mirror.ac.uk
The oddly-named Tucows has long been a great resource for Internet-related software, although it's been expanding to include other types of software too. Tucows

Downloading time depends in theory on the size of the file and the speed of your modem. In practice, this time also varies depending on how congested the site and network are.

To download shareware, you must:

1. Copy the file to a directory on your hard disk.

2. Decompress the file.

3. Install the program (run the file and follow the on-screen instructions).

The second step may not actually be necessary: you may be able to just double-click the file you downloaded to begin the installation. If the file is compressed, you will need a decompression

continued

program. Most shareware supplied for the PC is in the ZIP format, so you'll need a ZIP program such as WinZip (another shareware program, which you can download from **http://www.winzip.com**) *to decompress it. Macintosh files are often supplied in Stuffit (.sit) archives, and you'll need a program called Stuffit Expander (* **http://www.stuffit.com**) *to handle these.*

provides a simple search option on its homepage from which you can enter keywords and select the area to search from a drop-down list (a particular operating system, free themes, games, or children's software). This form of search uses the Boolean OR method, finding files whose descriptions contain any of the keywords you enter.

A **Super Search** link takes you to a separate page where your options are almost identical, with the addition of buttons letting you choose whether to search for all words, any word, or the exact phrase. (Like most software archives, you can ignore the search options and simply browse through categories of software if you prefer.)

Every file has a brief description, revision date and version number, download size, and a useful 'cow rating' where 5 cows means that this is 'best-of-breed' software.

Figure 6.9 Results of a search for 'screen saver' at Tucows.

Multimedia searches

7

Finding images

Finding maps

Finding images

It is not difficult to find images and, more generally, multimedia objects on the Web. Image and multimedia files are easily identified by their extension. It is easy to sort between:

- images in GIF format;
- images in JPEG format;
- sounds (.wav files);
- videos;
- animation.

*Using Windows, you can save an image displayed in your Internet browser by right-clicking on it, then selecting **Save image as**. When saving the image, you can rename it, choose a different format and choose the destination folder.*

GIF and JPEG are in fact the two formats most used on the Web. The GIF format records an image in 256 colours. Developed by Compuserve, it is a highly compact format which is well suited to transfers on slow-speed networks such as our good old switched telephone network. To obtain higher quality, use the compressed JPEG format (*Joint Picture Expert Group*). This format is better suited to transmitting high-quality photographic documents. But, in order not to slow down the loading of pages, images are sometimes presented in the form of small images, called 'thumbnails'. You can open the image on a new Web page in its true size and with the best possible quality just by clicking on it.

Image search engines

Image search engines allow you to scan the Web looking for illustrations, photos or rare documents. Be careful; if the documents retrieved are not free of charge, you will not be able to publish them yourself, unless you pay the author. But for your personal use, you can amuse yourself by collecting everything that interests you.

Webseek
http://www.ctr.columbia.edu/webseek/

This is an extraordinary tool from Columbia University in the United States. All image hunters should connect to this site in order to try it out. Webseek offers browsing by menu in addition to searching by criteria. Insofar as images are concerned, the result of your request is presented in the form of a page of thumbnails (see Figure 7.3), and the size of the original images is indicated. You can go to the site where the chosen image is located with just one click and open the image in its original size.

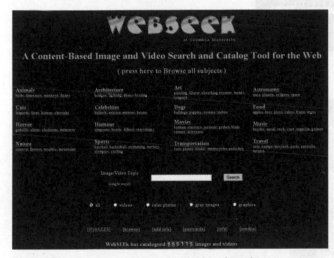

Figure 7.1 The home page with searching by subject.

The system allows you to find videos, black and white photos or colour photos. To do this, just check the appropriate box in the keyword text box.

The results are presented in the form of an electronic contact sheet: each corresponding document is displayed in the form of a small image. Then you just click on the image to access a document. The size of the actual image is displayed above the small image.

The service even allows you to find photos with similarities in terms of colours.

Figure 7.2 Searching by keyword and media type.

Figure 7.3 The result of a search.

Figure 7.4 The His command (histogram) allows you to search for similar shades.

Figure 7.5 Searching by subject: here, Arts – Painting, then Matisse.

Finding sounds on the Web

Lycos also allows you to find sound files. Take care to check the file formats (wav, midi, au or ra) and to ensure that you have the right software to listen to them. A number of sound documents broadcast are coded in ra format (for Real Audio) and can be processed by the Real Player software of the Progressive Networks company. This technique also allows sound to be broadcast live (live radio on the Web). Note that the Real Player program is included in Internet Explorer 4 and 5.

Lycos Image
http://www.lycos.co.uk/search/options.html

You discovered the general purpose search engine Lycos during Chapter 2, but the speciality of Lycos Image is, as its name suggests, that it finds images. To do this it uses a specialised analysis technique which is truly sophisticated. For example, the search engine allows you to find tourist images or photographs of well-known personalities.

Yahoo! Picture Gallery
http://gallery.yahoo.com/

You have already discovered Yahoo! UK and Ireland, then the international version of Yahoo!, and now here is Yahoo! Picture Gallery. This tools allows searching by keywords or from among the 12 categories offered (including arts, leisure, people, games, science and transport).

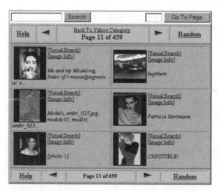

Figure 7.6 Searching by category; here a page on the top models.

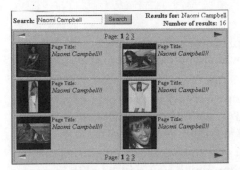

Figure 7.7 The request has been specified with the keyword 'Naomi Campbell'.

Once you have selected the category, a panel appears at random. You can specify the object of your search from the text box at the top of the screen.

Here again is a very efficient tool which image hunters should save in their Favorites.

Photo agencies

Photo agencies on the Web make a good starting point for browsing through images. These are professional sites offering the best negatives of the best photographers or offering high-quality images for sale. In order to protect themselves against abuse, images are displayed in low resolution and with limited colour palettes. In any case, it is not possible to display photographic-quality images on the Web, as the pass-band of networks is not suited to this. However, these documents may be offered for downloading.

Finding erotic sites

We cannot allude to searching for images without mentioning eroticism and pornography. If there is one domain where photographs are used in profusion, it is this one. And there is no shortage of such material on the Internet.

Do we need a search engine for this? Why not? Those who want to get down to the nitty gritty will be able to connect with **http://www. sexhunt.com/**.

Sygma Agency
http://www.sygma.fr/

The Sygma agency is one of the largest photo agencies in the world. The site presents a stock of over 700,000 images which you can download in high definition for a fee.

The results of a search by keyword are presented in the form of a contact sheet. By clicking on one of the images, you open the document in a separate window, and at the same time you obtain the photo's references.

You can also use online reports (Stories heading). News, People, Magazine and Illustration are the four sections from which you will be able to access recent photos.

Figure 7.8 Welcome to the Sygma agency.

Figure 7.9 The result of a search on the word 'portrait'.

Giraudon Agency
http://www.giraudon-photo.fr/

The Giraudon photographic agency has a unique base of 200,000 negatives and 70,000 ektachromes combining photographs in various categories including Decorative Arts, Celebrations, Mythology, The East, and Daily Life.

Searches are not carried out automatically on the Web. You must complete a form and indicate what you are looking for. The document base is particularly rich. If you are interested in Impressionism, more than 1,000 references are in stock. You can find almost 500 documents concerning Napoleon, for example.

Finding sounds or videos

For sound and video you can use the Lycos Multimedia service at **http://multi-media.lycos.com**. *As we also pointed out in Chapter 3, HotBot is an excellent tool for finding sound, video and even Shockwave animations.*

These animations use a Macromedia technique **(http:/www.macrome-dia.com**) *and you must first download the 'player' from this publisher's site in order to be able to view them on your PC.*

Figure 7.10 A photo is presented on request in a separate window.

And if laughter is the subject of your search, almost 100 documents from Gargantua to the Laughing Cow will be offered!

Finding maps

You have been able to see that some general search engines offer map searching. In addition there are sites which specialise in this type of search. If search engines are handy for getting you around cyberspace, maps and plans will be of use to you in getting back to earth!

Maps Database
http://www.internets.com/smaps.htm
This is a maps search engine which also offers a very full list of sites where maps can be found, with searching by category.

Xerox Map Viewer
http://pubweb.parc.xerox.com/map/color=1/features=alltypes
This software, developed by Xerox in 1993, allows you to discover the world interactively. Set the parameters of the visual representation software, click on the globe and discover the world. Latitude and longitude will no longer hold any secrets for you.

The Perry-Castenada Library Maps Collection
http://www.lib.utexas.edu/Libs/PCL/Map_collection/Map_collection.html
230,000 maps are listed and accessible from this address. There is something of everything here, and the map lover will be in his element. Maps are classified by continent and region. In addition, impressive lists are offered. On the menu are geographical maps, obviously, but also historical, political, economic maps, etc.

Lycos RoadMaps
http://www.proximus.com/lycos/
This is a remarkable service which displays the corresponding map from an address (street and town), with a cross indicating the street number requested. You can also title the map in order to personalise it and send it to a third party. Once the map has been displayed, it is possible to zoom in to obtain greater detail and discover all the surrounding services (hotels, restaurants, banks, etc.).

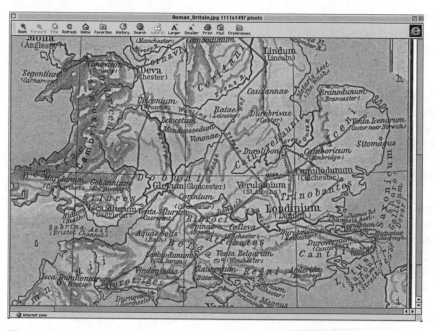

Figure 7.11 As an example, a map of Roman Britain from the historical atlas.

The Zoom In command allows you to obtain greater detail, while Zoom Out gives a more general overview of the place (just click on the graduated scale at the right of the map).

There is just one problem: this service only works in the United States. To make up for this, Lycos offers the City Guide service which you can reach by clicking the 'City Guide' link or by going to **http://cityguide.lycos.com**.

From a map of the world, you click on a continent, then, from the new map, on a country from the list displayed. From the country, you then access the map in question and a list of towns. For example, more than 60 English counties and cities are thus accessible, and there are thousands of towns and cities around the world which you can discover with a few clicks of the mouse. For each town or city, City Guide offers you a summary and a list of links used (culture, recreation, practical, etc.).

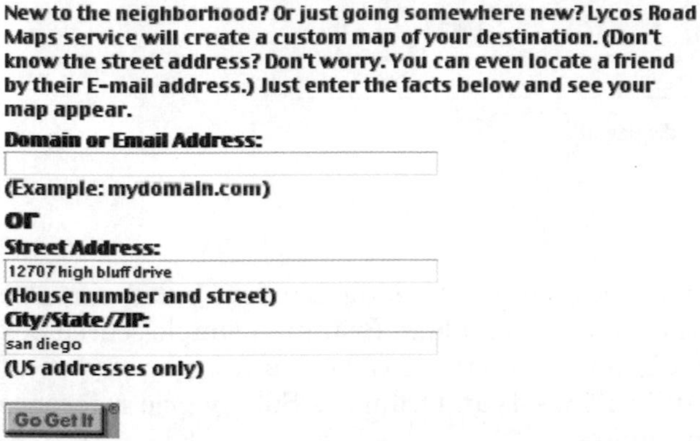

New to the neighborhood? Or just going somewhere new? Lycos Road Maps service will create a custom map of your destination. (Don't know the street address? Don't worry. You can even locate a friend by their E-mail address.) Just enter the facts below and see your map appear.

Domain or Email Address:

(Example: mydomain.com)

or

Street Address:

12707 high bluff drive

(House number and street)

City/State/ZIP:

san diego

(US addresses only)

Go Get It

Figure 7.12 Entering an address with Lycos RoadMaps.

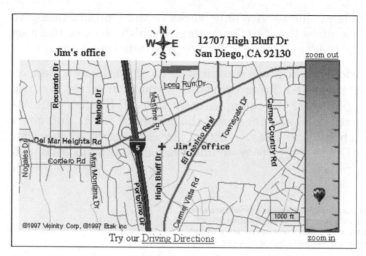

Figure 7.13 A personalised map is displayed.

UK Street Map Page
http://www.streetmap.co.uk

This site currently only has street maps for Greater London, but it can also provide road atlas maps for the whole of mainland Britain. A simple search box lets you search by entering a London street, a postcode, a town or city, or (if you prefer to do things the difficult way!) an Ordnance Survey grid reference or latitude and longitude coordinates.

By clicking on an area of the map you can centre the map on that grid square. The Zoom In/Zoom Out links let you view the centre of the current map in greater detail.

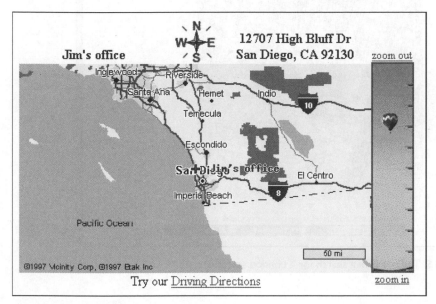

Figure 7.14 A more general view (Zoom Out).

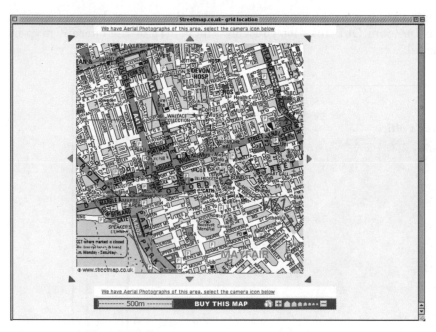

Figure 7.15 The result of a search for a London street.

Practical searches

Ferreting in virtual libraries

Window shopping on the Web!

From consulting a document to buying a product on the Web, everything starts with searching. The Web offers you virtual libraries and shops so that you can satisfy your thirst for knowledge or your hunger for consumption. To put it plainly, you can enrich yourself (intellectually) or spend without counting the cost!

Ferreting in virtual libraries

The hypertext technology, which was the main factor in designing the Web, was set up in order to easily exploit any kind of text document and to connect them by means of links. The written word occupies a place of honour on the Web, and you can find different types of document by browsing through the virtual libraries available.

Library of Congress
http://lcweb.loc.gov/
The Library of Congress contains more than 110 million documents in more than 400 languages. Most of the information in the library's catalogue is available online.

From the home page, the first search zone, American Memory, gives access to the following:

- text documents;
- photographic resources;
- the first films;
- sound documents.

From the Exhibition section you access the great exhibitions. Among these you'll be able to read transcriptions of the Gettysburg Address in 29 languages, find out how the American Declaration of Independence was drafted and read the first 'rough draft', or take a detour to the Vatican library with its own range of exhibits. Also discover the revelations of the Russian archives, or even, in another register, the discovery of America by Christopher Colombus in 1492. Or view on your PC the earliest map of California dating from 1562!

The library's services are detailed in Library Services. Here you will be able to access the virtual reading rooms. Twenty rooms await you with research

Figure 8.1 The home page of the largest virtual library in the world.

The search engine of the Library of Congress

Named LOCIS, it contains more than 27 million documents stored in different databases. Equipped with a real turbo, the library's catalogue contains not just its own documents but also other documents found in other libraries or research institutes. Among these documents, for example, you will find books, magazines, maps, music scores, films, posters, photographs or manuscripts. One file allows you to contact more than 13,000 research bodies throughout the world.

domains as varied as history, science, the arts, rare books or the cinema. For example, connect to the Early Motion Pictures page (1897–1916) to carry out research into early cinema productions.

It is in the Research section that you will find the search tools (Catalogue page/Research and Reference command).

The Catalogue page gives access to all search modes:

■ by word;

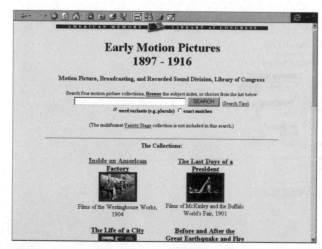

Figure 8.2 Searching for early films.

- by reference;
- by Boolean expression.

About a dozen additional search tools add to the basic mechanisms.

The British Library
http://www.bl.uk

The hub of the British library is Blaise, the British Library Automated Information Service, a collection of searchable databases containing over 19 million records which includes:

- the British Library Catalogue, which offers access to books published all over the world from 1450 to 1975;
- Whitaker, a weekly-updated database of British books published since 1965;
- Eighteenth Century Short Title Catalogue, records of all types of eighteenth-century printed materials;
- the Stationery Office, a database of government and official publications since 1976.

The full Blaise service is available by subscription, and the British Library Web site does little more than give a taste of what's available. However, the main database collections can be searched online without subscription using the OPAC 97 service.

Figure 8.3 Searching the British Library.

Internet Public Library

http://www.ipl.org/ref/

This is a virtual library which offers you hundreds of thousands of works and documents online. Choose a domain or a discipline from the home image, then refine your search until you find the exact subject that interests you. This service will display many online references and as many links with other sites containing information relating to your research.

Also click on the home image desk to ask a specific question. It can be very entertaining to consult the list of questions asked (with the answers). All kinds of things are there – how much is a 1983 Ford Fiesta worth? How much money did Yahoo! earn last year? Why is the sky blue? (Good question!)

This is another address which you should not miss.

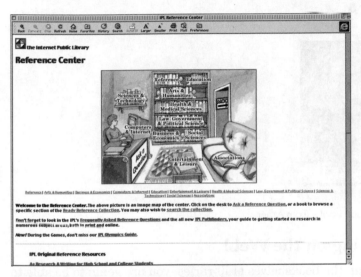

Figure 8.4 Welcome to Internet Public Library.

Athena
http://un2sg1.unige.ch/athena/html/athome.html
This virtual library created in Switzerland is the work of Pierre Perroud, lecturer in philosophy at the Collège Voltaire in Geneva. More than 3,700 literary texts are digitised, with the bonus of links with other consultation or downloading sites (**http://un2sg1.unige.ch/athena/html/booksite.html**).

Raffaello Sanzio (1483-1520) <u>Scuola di Atene.</u>

Je sème un grain qui pourra un jour produire une moisson.
Voltaire (1694 - 1778), <u>*Traité sur la Tolérance*</u> (1763).

Figure 8.5 Consult digitised books from Athena.

The Gutenberg Project is the most ambitious project underway on the Internet. Its objective is to digitise works and issue them via the Internet. Therefore the service is developing day by day, with new entries being added all the time. Dante's La Comédie is the 1,000th work thus digitised. It is accessible at the following addresses: **http://www. promo.net/pg, http://www.guten- berg. net** *or* **ftp://ftp. prairienet.org/pub/pr oviders/gutenberg** *(download site).*

Window shopping on the Web!

After ferreting through the bookshelves of libraries, you are going to be able to browse through the shelves and racks of the Web's virtual shops. And you will always be able to satisfy your hunger for knowledge by buying books!

While online shopping has been slow to develop in the UK, the United States is literally overflowing with this type of opportunity. And there is no shortage of shopping centres and different kinds of shop. Here too you need to find your feet and select the best services. The polemic surrounding payment guaranteed by bank card was inevitable, but one has to admit that it is no more risky today to buy online than to pay by credit card at a 'real' shop!

Our browsers now integrate the necessary functions for protected payment, so the risk of an ill-willed third party intercepting and using your card number, which is itself encrypted, is very slight.

Therefore you can buy (or rent) just about anything on the Net:

- products: books, clothing, cars;
- services: holiday lets;
- intangible products: electronic magazines, software, stock exchange transactions, etc.

Buying books

Books are some of the products best represented and most sold on the Net (other than computer products: hardware and software). You will have as much fun visiting these sites as ferreting in libraries. And as a bonus, you can order the works of your choice. Setting out to find an author, a forgotten title or a rare edition is a treat!

Waterstone's Online
http://www.waterstones.co.uk

One of the biggest names in High Street book sales is also on the Web, letting you browse titles by subject, read descriptions and buy online. You can carry out a simple search by typing the name of the author, book title or ISBN into the search field that appears on almost every page of the site. If this simple search doesn't turn up trumps, click the **Advanced Search** link. Advanced searches are made using any combination of:

- the author's name;
- the book's title;
- the subject;
- the ISBN;
- words descriptive of the book or subject;
- the publisher.

Figure 8.6 An 'Advanced Search' at Waterstone's.

When you find the book you want, you can order it instantly by clicking the **Add To Basket** link alongside its title.

Figure 8.7 The results of a search for fantasy writer Terry Pratchett.

BOL
http://www.uk.bol.com

BOL was originally a US store named Books On-Line. It now has country-specific versions for France, Germany, Sweden and many others as well as this UK store, and has added music, video and DVD to its range of products. You can select the type of product you want from the 'tabs' at the top of the homepage, or browse through BOL's subject categories. Alternatively, run a quick search by book title, author, keywords or ISBN using the drop-down menu and text box at the top of every page.

BOL uses an easy-to-follow shopping basket metaphor for online purchasing. Click the **Add To Basket** icon for any book you want to order. You can then choose to continue browsing or go to the checkout to provide delivery and payment details.

Figure 8.8 Run a quick search or browse by category at BOL.

iBS: The Internet Bookshop
http://www.bookshop.co.uk

iBS is part of the well-known High Street store WH Smith, and has one of the country's largest online bookstores with over 1.4 million UK and US titles. The usual options to browse by category or run a quick search are there, along with a Full Search option. This comprehensive search includes the usual search criteria (title, author, ISBN, publisher and series title), but also allows you to choose how the results should be presented, with options such as:

- Price (cheapest first);
- Alphabetically by Title;
- Publication date (most recent first).

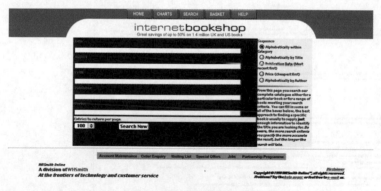

Figure 8.9 The Full Search page at iBS.

Amazon.com

http://www.amazon.co.uk

With more than 2.5 million books online, Amazon has become the indisputable reference point for anybody wanting to buy a book on the Web. Even the rarest editions or books which are out of print are sold, although the service requires six months to track down a rare work. When the book is found, a price quotation will be sent by e-mail. You can then decide whether or not to buy the work in question.

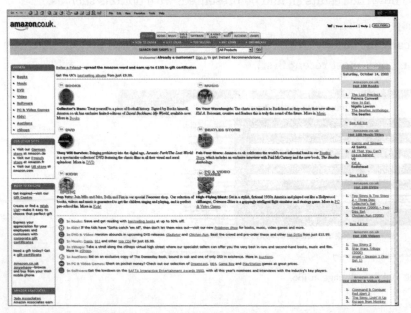

Figure 8.10 Welcome to Amazon, the largest virtual bookshop on the Web.

Research is by keyword or subject. Readers can give their opinion on a work, just like authors and publishers, which is an excellent way of enriching the information base.

Amazon offers numerous services, some of which are as commonplace as choosing the wrapping paper for a gift. But it is these little extras that end up making a site a success.

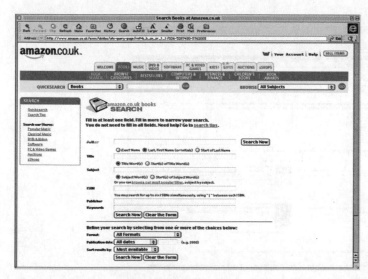

Figure 8.11 The search data entry form using Amazon.co.uk.

Barnes and Noble
http://www.barnesandnoble.com/

With more than one million references, the virtual shop window of the famous publisher is highly attractive.

As always, searching is by category, title or author's name, or even by keyword. Just check the box of a work to add it to your virtual trolley before entering ordering mode.

Figure 8.12 The home page of the Barnes and Noble virtual bookshop.

Search: Books
_____

Please select at least one search criteria.
Fill in one or more of the fields below:
Title of Book

Author's Name
Cave, Nick|
Keywords

[▶ Search]   [Clear Fields]   ▶ Search Tips

You can narrow your search by selecting one or more options below:

Price   Format
[all prices   ⬍]   [all formats   ⬍]

Age   Subjects
[all age ranges   ⬍]   [all subjects   ⬍]

_____

You can also search by ISBN
ISBN

[   ]   [▶ Search ISBN]

Figure 8.13 The Barnes and Noble books search engine.

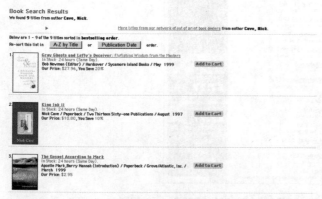

Book Search Results
We found 9 titles from author Cave, Nick.

          ▶   More titles from our network of out of print book dealers from author Cave, Nick.

Below are 1 – 9 of the 9 titles sorted in **bestselling order**.
Re-sort this list in [A-Z by Title] or [Publication Date] order.

1. **Gray Ghosts and Lefty's Deceiver:** *Flyfishing Wisdom from the Masters*
    In Stock: 24 hours (Same Day).
    Bob Newman (Editor) / Hardcover / Sycamore Island Books / May 1999   [Add to Cart]
    Our Price: $27.96, You Save 20%

2. **King Ink II**
    In Stock: 24 hours (Same Day).
    Nick Cave / Paperback / Two Thirteen Sixty-one Publications / August 1997   [Add to Cart]
    Our Price: $10.80, You Save 10%

3. **The Gospel According to Mark**
    In Stock: 24 hours (Same Day).
    Apostle Mark, Barry Hannah (Introduction) / Paperback / Grove/Atlantic, Inc. /   [Add to Cart]
    March 1999
    Our Price: $2.95

Figure 8.14 The result of a search at Barnes and Noble.

Using the traditional search engines to find shops

For example, Web Crawler (**http://webcrawler.com /Shopping/**) offers a search of online shopping sites. You thus have hundreds of virtual shops at the click of a mouse, classified by product type. You can find many popular shops: Barnes and Noble for books, Disney Store, CD Now, etc.

Figure 8.15 The home page of the Shops On The Net shopping directory.

Shops On The Net
http://www.shopsonthenet.co.uk
Hundreds of virtual shops at the click of a mouse button. Browse through 34 categories of shops and services, or run a quick keyword search for either a particular shop or a product by clicking the appropriate button beside the search field.

UK Shopping City
http://www.ukshops.co.uk/enter.shtml
The UK Shopping City is a large virtual shopping centre with a number of areas including Retail, Travel and Property. You can browse by selecting an area and touring the different levels of the shopping centre where you'll find some of the biggest High Street names, including Marks and Spencer, Interflora, Argos, Comet and Dixons.

Figure 8.16 Level I of the UK Shopping City's Retail area.

'Surfing' guides

9

How to surf

Discovering Web site compilations and guides

Visiting top sites

Browsing the whole world

Searching in any language

How to surf

Surfing isn't a search method in the strict sense, of course, but surfing guides make good starting points for finding the best Web sites. This process clearly relies much more on trial and error, or pure luck, but if you find the precision of search queries tiresome, let yourself be guided and ride the wave!

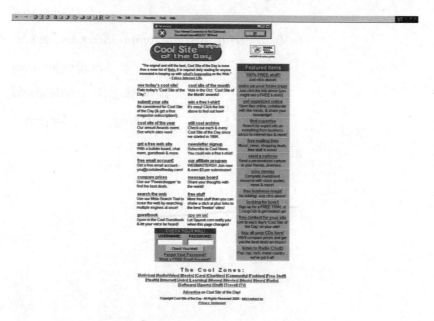

Figure 9.1 The Cool Site of the Day home page.

Cool Site of the Day
http://cool.infi.net/
This selection, made by Glenn Davis of Infinet, is without doubt one of the best starting points on the Web. Each day you can discover a new 'Cool Site'.

Excite Search Voyeur
http://www.excite.com/search/voyeur
Excite's Search Voyeur service displays a list of 10 queries that users are currently searching for at Excite. This list automatically updates every 30 seconds to bring you constant selections of the latest searches. If any search query seems interesting, just click it to run the same search yourself. An ideal way to add a touch of adventure to your surfing!

Figure 9.2 Let yourself by guided by Excite Search Voyeur.

Compilations to visit
- *Top 50 UK Web Sites:*
  http://www.top50.co.uk

- *PC Magazine's Top 100:*
  http://www.zdnet.com/pcmag/special/web100

- *The Weekly Hot 100:*
  http://www.100hot.com

Discovering Web site compilations and guides

Guides offer rational surfing. They generally include access by subject and search tools. On the Web, everybody, or nearly everybody, draws up lists of sites to visit and all this may more or less resemble a guide. You will find lists of good addresses on the home pages of other surfers. In the light of this profusion of guides, which we have had the opportunity to present during previous chapters, we have decided to be restrained (for once!) and provide you with just one good address.

MSN Directory
http://search.msn.co.uk

The MSN Directory, published by Microsoft, lists hundreds of top sites for UK surfers in over 50 categories. To browse the directory after arriving at this page, either choose one of the major categories (in bold type) to see the top picks, or select a subcategory (in plain type) to see sites specific to that category.

In many of the categories you'll find not only links to top Web sites but direct links to the top news stories in the national or computing press, reviews of the latest computing products, special offers from UK shopping sites, and many other time-saving links.

Visiting top sites

On the Web you will find all kinds of Web site classification, such as:

- classifications carried out by surfers who choose the best sites;
- classifications prepared by professional teams (cyber-journalists);

Figure 9.3 Hundreds of ready-sorted links and searches at MSN Directory.

■ classifications prepared by software based on how often a site is visited, generally known as hits.

Here are two examples:

Lycos Top 5%

http://www.pointcom.com/

The best of the Web by the Lycos team.

Figure 9.4 Lycos' Top 5%.

Figure 9.5 The Top10Links page.

Top10Links
http://www.top10links.com
The best sites on the Web in over 1,000 ready-sorted categories.

Browsing the whole world

You have had the opportunity to travel the world using the large international search engines. If you want to go further still on your trip into cyberspace, there is an impressive number of specialist tools which will take you from one country to another with ease. A world tour in the space of a few clicks!

Matilda
http://www.aaa.com.au/images/logos/searches/world/
This travelling search engine comes to us from Australia. With more than 200 countries listed and endowed with specific search mechanisms for each of them, Matilda is worth discovering.

You will be astonished to note that lists of hits provide very specific information, including the target audience and even the site's popularity!

Woyaa!
Http://www.woyaa.com
Woyaa! is a specialist search engine for Africa, with subject entries (arts, society, culture, etc.) or keyword searching. A considerable number of sites are listed, and if you want to carry out research into the African continent, this is where to start.

Figure 9.6 The choice of countries offered by Matilda.

Figure 9.7 Searching by country with Matilda; in this case, Benin.

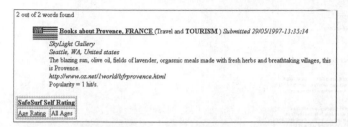

> 2 out of 2 words found
>
> 🇺🇸 **Books about Provence, FRANCE** (Travel and **TOURISM**) *Submitted 29/05/1997-13:35:34*
>
> *SkyLight Gallery*
> *Seattle, WA, United states*
> The blazing sun, olive oil, fields of lavender, orgasmic meals made with fresh herbs and breathtaking villages, this is Provence.
> *http://www.oz.net/1world/bfrprovence.html*
> Popularity = 1 hit/s.
>
> **SafeSurf Self Rating**
> | Age Rating | All Ages |

Figure 9.8 An answer from Matilda.

As a bonus, the site offers you Net Radio Earthbeat so you can surf to music!

Figure 9.9 The home page of the African search engine Woyaa!

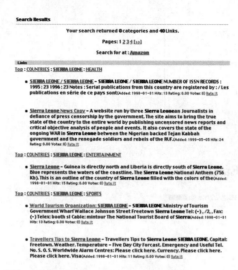

Figure 9.10 The result of a search on the keyword 'Sierra Leone'.

The Virtual Tourist
http://www.vtourist.com/webmap/
Click on the globe and then on the map of the region of the world selected. You then access specific resources for the country chosen, in English or in the language of the country in question.

Figure 9.11 Click on the world map to access a continent or a country.

Figure 9.12 Access to Europe.

Figure 9.13 Here, access to the countries of South America.

Searching in any language

What we offer here is a selection of languages and sites. A quick tour of the Web to allow you to glimpse its wealth. Also, you must set the parameters of your browser for it to correctly display the characters of the various languages.

In all languages

EuroSeek

http://www.euroseek.net/page?ifl=uk

This is a remarkable search tool which allows you to target a search on a given country and also to choose the answers (target sites) in the language of your choice. 40 languages are offered, classified in alphabetical order from Bulgarian (Balgarski) to Turkish (Türkçe)!

Figure 9.14 Searching throughout all the countries and in all the languages of Europe.

In English, for non-English speaking countries
Russia on the Net
http://www.ru/
The home page of Russia on the Net is shown in Figure 9.15.

Figure 9.15 Searching sites in Russia.

Jewish Communication Network
http://www.jcn18.com/scripts/jcn18/paper/query.asp

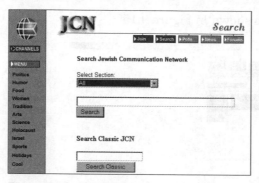

Figure 9.16 A search tool for the Jewish community.

Indonesia Net
http://www.indonesianet.com/search.htm

Figure 9.17 Searching in Indonesia.

In Austrian
Austrian Home Page Search Engine
http://www.aco.net/Server-in-AT/
Plain text searching.

Figure 9.18 Searching for Austrian sites.

Austronaut
http://austronaut.at/url.ims
Searching by URL or keyword.

In Danish
Jubii
http://www.jubii.dk
Searching by keyword and by subject.

Figure 9.19 Searching in Danish.

In Spanish
University of Cordoba
http://www.uco.es/

In Portuguese
University of Aveiro
http://www.ua.pt/

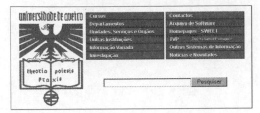

Figure 9.20 Searching in Portuguese.

Searching the media

Getting back to the source with press agencies

Rummaging through newspapers and magazines

Searching the international media

Searching in the media is a highly efficient way of finding information on the Web. Here 'media' is taken to mean all the traditional large-scale media (press, radio, television) with Web links, but also cybermedia which have developed on the Web.

Having made this distinction, it must be said that the traditional media have managed to assert themselves on the Web, while many cybermedia have yet to prove themselves.

Online media offer the latest news items and also open up their archives for searching. A new track for finding information!

Getting back to the source with press agencies

If you are interested in current affairs, start here. You can obtain information well before the evening television news. And above all, you can find dispatches from all over the world. On the Internet, you choose what you want to receive, and you are not governed by the choices made by professionals in the world of communications. But beware, some services are, quite legitimately, subject to a fee.

Ananova
http://www.ananova.com
This UK Press Association Web site should be your first port of call to find the latest national, international and business news stories. A 'StoryFinder' service allows you to run a keyword search for news articles, optionally selecting an area of the UK or a particular topic to narrow the search.

Figure 10.1 Catch the breaking news stories first at Ananova.

Reuters
http://www.reuters.com
This is one of the largest press agencies in the world, and the service offered by the Web is high quality. The options for searching by subject are particularly attractive. For this you use the drop-down list above the Products button.

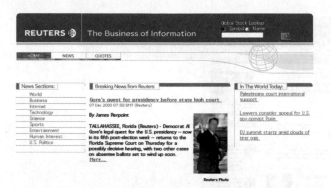

Figure 10.2 The Reuters agency opens its doors to you.

Figure 10.3 Searching for sports news items.

Computer Wire
http://www.computerwire.com/
Computer Wire is a press agency specialising in information technology (IT). The site even allows you to create your personalised information letter. The Search tool allows you to search using several criteria in the archives of magazines devoted to computers and telecommunications.

Figure 10.4 Searching through the archives with Computer Wire.

Finding press agencies with Yahoo!

To go even further, you can use Yahoo! to ask for a list of the world's press agencies. The address is: **http://dir. yahoo.com/Business_ and_Economy/Business _to_Business/News_and _Media/News_Service.**

Rummaging through newspapers and magazines

If you want to find a news item or article, then consult the Web sites of the large dailies and explore their archives when they are available online. You can even set up electronic press reviews. You need to identify good sources and learn to rummage around, searching by criteria or in plain text mode (the technique of indexing all significant words contained in an article). Head for the archives!

The Electronic Telegraph
http://www.telegraph.co.uk
The online edition of the popular *Daily Telegraph* allows searching of its news archives dating back to 1994, along with separate databases covering travel

reports and book reviews. To use this service, you will first need to register with the site. Registration is quick and free, and simply involves providing some personal details. You can then choose a personal user name and password which provide access to the archives.

The search options allow you to:

■ search for names (using initial capitals) or keywords;

■ specify a particular year, month or date;

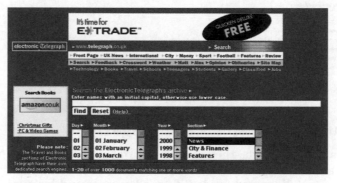

Figure 10.5 Searching for articles in the Electronic Telegraph.

■ narrow your search to a single section.

When searching by section, you can hold down the **Ctrl** key to select multiple sections for searching.

Results are presented in a list comprising:

■ the date;

■ the headline of the article; and

■ a relevance score in percent.

Just click on the headline to open the article.

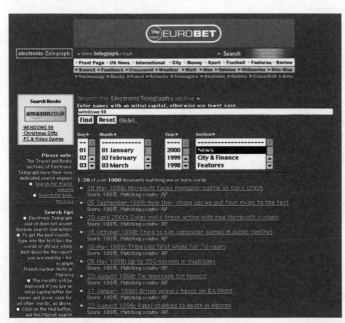

Figure 10.6 The results of an Electronic Telegraph search using the keywords 'Windows 98'.

The Times
http://www.thetimes.co.uk

As the search page itself explains, there are four ways to search The Times. Simple and Advanced searches let you search the current edition of The Times online; an Archive search allows searching for articles in past issues; and a Back Issues search helps you find an entire online edition.

The Guardian/The Observer
http://www.guardian.co.uk

Although its archives date back only to September 1998, The Guardian's search options are more powerful than those of some of its rivals. Searches automatically cover both Guardian and Observer archives in the period you

Figure 10.7 Search Guardian and Observer archives using Boolean and case-sensitive keywords.

select, and results can be sorted by date or by relevance to your keywords. You can also choose to display only the first paragraph of matching articles, making it easy to see whether you've found what you were looking for.

The Financial Times
http://www.ft.com
Visit the TotalSearch section of the site to search over 10 million articles from a number of business and financial sources dating back to 1996. Among the many search options available, you can:

Figure 10.8 The world's financial news at your fingertips, courtesy of the Financial Times.

- choose whether to search in articles' headlines, text or both;
- choose the types of publication to search or pick a single publication (such as the FT itself) from a list of over 3,000;
- search a particular financial sector (such as Banking or Media);
- search by region (such as UK & Ireland or North America).

Searching the international media

There are thousands of titles to discover on the Web. It is not easy to find your way, but information is there somewhere. Here too we will restrict ourselves to a selection of the main titles on the Web (such as *The Washington Post*), or new media (such as MSNBC). While traditional media are sometimes reproached for giving disinformation, one could accuse the Web of over-information. For this reason the search tools and filters which it allows you to use are helpful. That is also why it may be useful to target a few good addresses to serve as a starting point for looking for specific information.

MSNBC
http://www.msnbc.com/
Born out of collaboration between ABC and MSN (Microsoft Network), as soon as you reach the site MSNBC offers to install a news browser. This plug-in for your browser will be of use to you in looking at international current affairs.

Beware: you will need a fast computer in order to benefit fully from this very multimedia site.

Figure 10.9 Welcome to MSNBC.

The Washington Post
http://www.washingtonpost.com/
When you have the front page online, you can:

- select a section from the drop-down list;
- activate the paper's index;
- start the search engine.

It is best to search for articles over the last fortnight, but you can restrict this time band.

The search page also gives access to:

■ the news dispatches of the AP (Associated Press) agency;

■ a multitude of databases in the business, leisure and entertainment domain.

You can also search for news by country. 220 countries are listed and if you type 'France', for example, you will access a front page relating to France which is particularly rich. You can also travel the entire world!

Figure 10.10 The Washington Post home page.

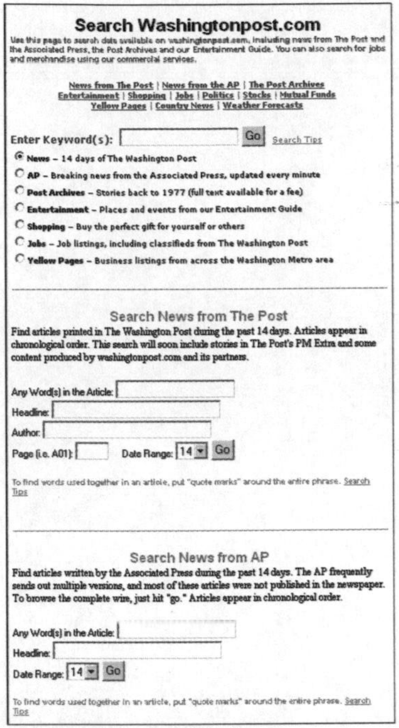

Figure 10.11 Searching for articles in The Washington Post.

The Chicago Tribune
http://www.chicago.tribune.com/
The Chicago Tribune is another heavyweight of the media with sophisticated search tools. The online version allows you to search its archives going back to 1985.

An international video-tex service on your PC!

Webdo, a Swiss magazine, offers an impressive list of online media (**http://www.presseweb.ch**). *You search by country and have access to thousands of titles! Also take a close look at Chaplin's News* (**http://www. geocities. com/Heartland/ 2308/**). *The list of subjects is impressive.*

Use Net Media (**http://www.go-public.com/netmedia/**) *if you want to search by country.*

Or again, with classification by country, The Inkternational News Link (**http://inkpot.com/news/**).

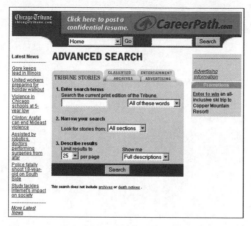

Figure 10.12 Searching for articles in the Chicago Tribune.

You can ask for the following results to be sorted:

- date;
- relevance;
- frequency of appearance of the keyword.

You can search in relation to a specific year, or search through all the archives. It is possible in this way to obtain nearly 3,000 published articles which include the word 'Microsoft'. For each article you get a summary. You will have to click the heading in order to obtain the full version.

'Push' technologies

Using personalised newspapers

Receiving information by e-mail

While we have learned to 'pull' information from the Web in the first ten chapters of this book, the final chapter will be devoted to push techniques. This time we do not go to the information, the information comes to us; it is 'pushed' onto our PC.

This method of receiving information adds a few new possibilities to the way you use the Web. You can:

- define your own preferences and receive personalised newspapers and magazines containing only what interests you;
- have information delivered automatically by e-mail;
- use helper applications and other intelligent programs which ferret through the Web for you.

With 'push' technologies, the Web is trying to match the media (which broadcast information), but the major difference between push and pull technology is that with push, the information may be personalised. This is one of the key aspects of service and media on the Internet.

Using personalised newspapers

Consulting a newspaper whose front page and articles are intended for you personally is not just a dream. On the Web there are many services which allow you to define your tastes and preferences. Knowing your profile, these services will then be able to deliver truly personalised information.

Crayon
http://crayon.net/
With Crayon, step by step you can construct your own live daily newspaper free of charge. Choose a password, and then proceed with the choice of a title, formatting, headings, links with information sources, etc.

Two design modes are available:

- standard mode, which scans all information sources in detail;
- quick mode, for the basics (it uses American zip codes to deliver regional information to US users).

By preference use standard mode and select:

- headings (world, tech, science, religion, Web, etc.) by clicking on the colour crayons at the foot of the page;
- information sources included under a heading by checking the media which interest you.

You can also add your suggested information sources. Finally, click on the **'Create my own newspaper now'** button when you are ready!

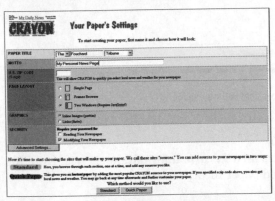

Figure 11.1 Crayon is useful for personalising your newspaper.

Then select the hierarchy of your headings (the different sections about which you have already given information). Click on '**Publish my newspaper**' and it is done. The paper can be consulted immediately. Do not forget to save the page in your Favorites in order to access it easily in future.

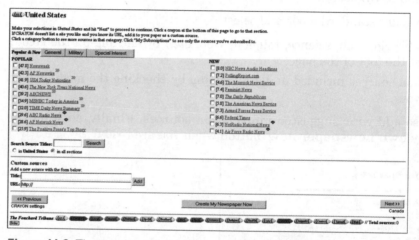

Figure 11.2 The interactive design of a personalised newspaper.

MyYahoo
http://edit.my.yahoo.com/config/login
The famous search engine also offers an *à la carte* information service. Here too you can create your own personalised paper incorporating, for example:

■ stock exchange information;

The Fouchard Tribune
"My Personal News Page"

≡ Read My Front Page

<Modify this paper>

World
[Edit]
--- BBC World News

Business
[Edit]
≡ *Business Week* Daily Briefing

InfoTech
[Edit]
--- PC Magazine
≡ Wired News
--- WebWeek

Web Spotlight
[Edit]
--- Cool Central Site of the Day

United States
[Edit]
--- Newsweek

Figure 11.3 The front page of a personal newspaper.

- sports results;
- international current affairs;
- Web resources;
- and much more!

Follow the step-by-step instructions. From weather reports to computers via sports or television, the list of headings is enormous. Then, MyYahoo takes care of the content and you just have to plug into your daily newspaper. If you are permanently connected to the Internet, you can receive information on your desk in real time. Otherwise, you can download software, News Ticker, which will enable you to access the information with just one click.

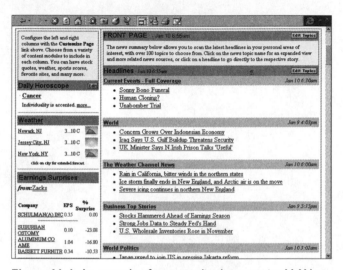

Figure 11.4 An example of a personalised paper using MyYahoo.

Excite

http//www.excite.com/Info/

Yahoo! is not the only search engine that tracks down information for you. Excite offers a similar service with 14 subject channels at your disposal. After identifying yourself, you choose your channels. The Web pages offered can be customised to your requirements.

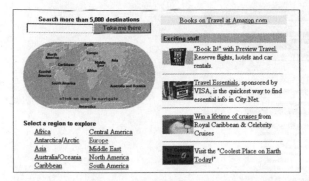

Figure 11.5 Searching Excite's Travel channel – 5,000 possible destinations!

News Tracker
http://nt.excite.com/

This is a new service with the Excite hallmark, which allows you to keep track of current affairs. This gigantic information service compiles more than 300 sources. All current affairs are covered, including computer news. As with a search engine, you can search for information by indicating a few keywords. You can create your 'personalised newspaper' by defining your areas of interest.

NewsHub
http://www.newshub.com/tech/

This is not, strictly speaking, a personalised newspaper. NewsHub will track down the titles of the largest information sources in the hi-tech domain every 15 minutes. If you want a lower frequency, you can indicate this under Preferences.

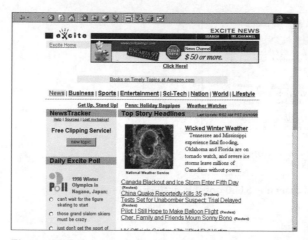

Figure 11.6 An extract from the News Tracker search page.

Thus, NewsHub gathers only computer news by scanning information that you can find on sites such as Yahoo!'s Tech, Nando InfoTech, Tec Wire, Gina I-Wire, InfoWorld, PC Week, ZD-net, ComputerWorld or Wired, to name but a few.

Receiving information by e-mail

A very easy way of tracking down information is to subscribe to e-mail delivery services, of which there are many on the Web. Use them, as they are often very helpful. But do not overuse them or your mail box will be snowed under. You can always cancel a subscription by sending a command along the lines of 'unsubscribe' to the server.

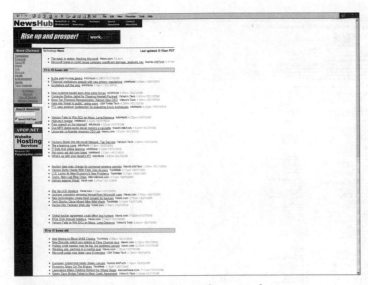

Figure 11.7 NewsHub tracks down information for you.

InBox Direct
http://home.netscape.com/ibd

This service offered by Netscape, the publisher of the browser with the same name, allows you to receive information directly to your e-mail in-box. You just have to choose the publications, classified by heading, which interest you. They will then be delivered to you by e-mail in HTML format. Just check that your messaging software accepts this format (the latest generation software does accept this format, e.g. Netscape Communicator and Internet Explorer 4.0 or 5.0).

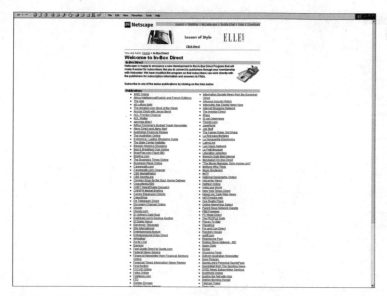

Figure 11.8 The home page of the InBox Direct messaging service.

Slate

http://www.slate.com

This magazine, which belongs to Microsoft, was not designed to relay computer news. It is a general magazine which covers politics as well as culture or leisure.

You can use Slate in three ways:

■ just consult the Web site;

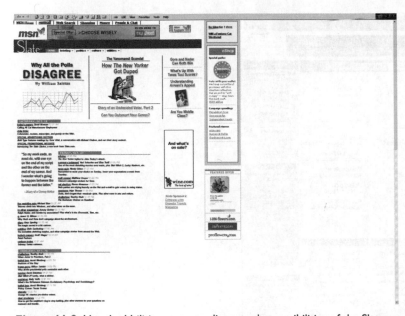

Figure 11.9 Use the Utilities menu to discover the possibilities of the Slate magazine.

- leave your e-mail and you will receive the titles of the articles when they appear. This enables you to go to the site only when you have found interesting articles;
- ask to automatically receive the full edition of Slate in your mail box. You will then receive a file in Word format which you can consult on screen or print.

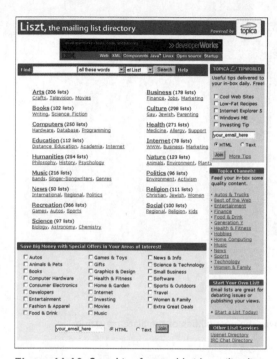

Figure 11.10 Searching for worldwide mailing lists.

International mailing lists

To find international mailing lists, visit the Listz site **(http://www.liszt.com)**. It offers more than 80,000 mailing lists. You can search by keyword or by subject. Also worth a visit is the Publicly Availably Mailing Lists site at **http://www. paml.net.**

Index